WONDERDADS

THE BEST DAD/CHILD ACTIVITIES IN ANN ARBOR

CONTACT WONDERDADS

WonderDads books may be purchased for educational and promotional use. For information, please email us at store@wonderdads.com.

If you are interested in partnership opportunities with WonderDads, please email us at partner@wonderdads.com.

If you are interested in selling WonderDads books and other products in your region, please email us at hiring@wonderdads.com.

For corrections, recommendations on what to include in future versions of the book, updates or any other information, please email us at info@wonderdads.com.

ISBN: 978-1-935153-72-6
First Printing, 2011
10 9 8 7 6 5 4 3 2 1

WONDERDADS
ANN ARBOR
Table of Contents

WELCOME TO WONDERDADS ANN ARBOR

Like so many other Dads, I love being with my kids, but struggle to find the right work/home balance. We are a part of a generation where Dads play much more of an active role with their kids, yet the professional and financial strains are greater than ever. We hope that the ideas in this book make it a little easier to be inspired to do something that makes you a hero in the eyes of your children.

This part of our children's lives goes by too fast, but the memories from a WonderDads inspired trip, event, meal, or activity last a long time (and will probably be laughed about when they grow up). So plan a Daddy day once a week, make breakfast together every Saturday morning, watch your football team every Sunday, or whatever works for you, and be amazed how long they will remember the memories and how good you will feel about yourself in the process.

Our warmest welcome to WonderDads.

Sincerely,

Jonathan Aspatore, **Founder & Dad**
Charlie (4) and Luke (3)

THE TOP 10 OVERALL BEST DAD/CHILD THINGS TO DO

TOP 5 DAD/CHILD RESTAURANTS

TOP 5 DAD/CHILD ACTIVITIES

TOP 5 DAD/CHILD
OUTDOOR PARKS & RECREATION

TOP 5 DAD/CHILD THINGS
TO DO ON A RAINY DAY

THE BEST DAD/CHILD
RESTAURANTS

AFTERNOON DELIGHT
Angell

251 East Liberty St.
Ann Arbor, MI 48104

(734) 665-7513 | www.afternoondelightcafe.com

Afternoon Delight is a great place to have breakfast in downtown Ann Arbor, and a great place to make THE place you take the kids for brunch.

ASHLEY'S RESTAURANT
Angell

338 South State St.
Ann Arbor, MI 48104

(734) 996-9191 | www.ashleys.com

Ashley's has been a part of downtown Ann Arbor's food tradition since 1983. They have a dad's-wallet-pleasing kids' menu that's fun for everyone. The children's menu features create-your-own personal pizza for $3.99 and a dinosaur chicken nugget and fries entrée also for $3.99. Ashley's also has a little something, something for dad, too.

BD'S MONGOLIAN GRILL
Angell

200 South Main St.
Ann Arbor, MI 48104

(734) 913-0999 | www.gomongo.com

This is a unique dining experience. You can create your own stir-fry using meat, seafood, vegetables, and various seasonings and sauces, which are cooked on a large, flat grill. It's all you can eat and they also have a salad bar.

COTTAGE INN PIZZA
Angell

512 East William St.
Ann Arbor, MI 48104

(734) 663-3379 | www.cottageinn.com

Cottage Inn makes above-average pizza pies, that greatest of kid pleasers, and is competitively priced.

FRASER'S PUB
Angell

2045 Packard St.
Ann Arbor, MI 48104

(734) 665-1955 | www.fraserspubaa.com

Fraser's Pub is an economically priced family restaurant which now serves breakfast on the weekends. They have a very nice children's menu with deals starting at $2.99. Be the dad who knows a good deal when he sees one.

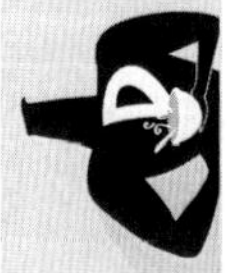

GANDY DANCER

Angell

401 Depot St.
Ann Arbor, MI 48104
(734) 769-0592 | www.muer.com

As a history buff I thoroughly enjoyed my stroll down memory lane. The Gandy Dancer is a fully restored historic train depot which serves fine cuisine in a high-class atmosphere. A truly novel experience no dad and son/daughter should be without.

MEDITERRANO

Angell

2900 South State St.
Ann Arbor, MI 48104
(734) 332-9700 | www.mediterrano.com

Ann Arbor is filled with fine international dining establishments. Mediterrano's is an excellent example of fine European cuisine. They feature cuisines from France, Greece, Spain and North Africa. This restaurant would be an excellent way to introduce foods from all over the world to your sons' or daughters' paletes.

REAL SEAFOOD COMPANY

Angell

341 South Main St.
Ann Arbor, MI 48104
(734) 769-5960 | www.realseafoodcorestaurant.com

The Real Seafood Company restaurant is a seafood lover's dream. The pictures on the website alone look good enough to eat, but just wait until you can smell and taste your dish! The restaurant's menu features a wide variety of seafood selections that won't break the bank. This is an absolute must-visit for all dads wanting to expose their sons or daughters to cuisines from all over the world. Absent a trip to Maine to catch your own lobster, you might want to try this restaurant out.

SHALIMAR

Angell

307 South Main St.
Ann Arbor, MI 48104
(734) 663-1500 | www.shalimarrestaurant.com

Shalimar is an authentic Indian restaurant which features a wide range of cuisine but specializes in foods that include North Indian, Tandoori and Mughlai dishes. Be the dad who adds a taste of India to your child's soon to be educated palete. There's always the simplicity of rice, naan and vegetable samosas for younger eaters.

BELLA CIAO TRATTORIA
Bach

118 West Liberty St.
Ann Arbor, MI 48104

(734) 995-2107

Downtown Ann Arbor offers great Italian restaurants. Since 1987, Bella Ciao Trattoria has been one of them. In addition to offering seasonal specialties featuring local ingredients, their house specialties are saffron lobster ravioli with grilled onion sauce and beef tenderloin with brandy sauce.

D'AMATO'S NEIGHBORHOOD RESTAURANT
Bach

102 South First St.
Ann Arbor, MI 48104

(734) 623-7400 | www.damatos.com

D'Amato's Neighborhood Restaurant offers delicious Italian cuisine in a bistro—style setting. Some of my favorite meals include filet mignon and chicken Marsala. Be the dad who knows where to go for great Italian cuisine.

GRATZI
Bach

326 South Main St.
Ann Arbor, MI 48104

(888) 456-3463 | www.gratzirestaurant.com

Ann Arbor is known for having great restaurants with great ambience. Gratzi is just such a place. It is a true dining experience you've got to try at least once. It's a special occasion just to go here, so you may as well go for a special occasion. Definitely call ahead for reservations.

GRIZZLY PEAK BREWING COMPANY
Bach

120 West Washington St.
Ann Arbor, MI 48104

(734) 741-7325 | www.grizzlypeak.net

Take my kids to a brewing company, you say? Definitely, when that brewpub has a kid-friendly menu of burgers, fries, wood-fired pizzas, grilled cheese, and macaroni & cheese. Loud and friendly, with lots of families every night.

PAESANO'S ITALIAN RESTAURANT AND WINE BAR
Bach

3411 Washtenaw Ave.
Ann Arbor, MI 48104

(734) 971-0484 | www.paesanosannarbor.com

Paesano's is a casual dining restaurant that features authentic regional Italian cuisine.

PALIO

Bach

347 South Main St.
Ann Arbor, MI 48104
(734) 668-6062 | www.paliorestaurant.com

Delicious food is something to be savored. Be the dad who increases his child's culinary palete. Palio offers traditional Italian roadside cooking in a comfortable dining atmosphere.

ZINGERMAN'S DELI

Bach

422 Detroit St.
Ann Arbor, MI 48104
(734) 663-3354 | www.zingermansdeli.com

Zingerman's is a delicious historic Ann Arbor landmark. A dad would be remiss in his hero duties if he never took the kids to Zingerman's. The sandwiches are inventive, delicious and original.

KRAZY JIM'S BLIMPY BURGERS

Burns Park–Central

551 South Division St.
Ann Arbor, MI 48104
(734) 663-4590 | www.blimpyburgers.com

Krazy Jim's has been an Ann Arbor favorite since 1953. It's known for having the best burgers around. The formula is simple, the meat is ground fresh and the portions are huge. They only serve single burgers to children. Krazy Jim's is also known for variety. They claim to have 2,147,483,648 possible combination of Blimpy burgers. Be the dad who knows a good burger when he eats one.

PIZZA HOUSE

Burns Park–Central

618 Church St.
Ann Arbor, MI 48104
(734) 995-5095 | www.pizzahouse.com

Be the dad who knows that pizza offers all of the food groups. Maybe not, but it is a favorite for most children. The Pizza House offers an excellent Chicago-style pizza and other Italian cuisines. The restaurant is located in the heart of downtown Ann Arbor.

PRICKLY PEAR CAFÉ

Burns Park–Central

328 South Main St.
Ann Arbor, MI 48104
(734) 930-0047 | www.pricklypearcafe.com

The Prickly Pear opened in 1991 and has been a favorite dining destination for food lovers who crave Southwestern cuisine. All the reviews say the food is delicious and the portions are more than ample. Their specialties include a butternut squash soup and a buffalo enchilada.

AHMO'S GYROS AND DELI
Eberwhite

341 East Huron St.
Ann Arbor, MI 48104

(734) 662-4445 | www.ahmosgyrosanddeli.com

Need a quick bite and Greek is what you seek? Then Ahmo's is the place to eat. Besides the very popular chicken gyros they also serve grilled cheese sandwiches and hot dogs and a full range of healthy dishes like creamy hummus, grape leaf rolls and freshly tossed salads. Be the dad who makes the healthy call.

ALI BABA
Eberwhite

601 Packard St.
Ann Arbor, MI 48104

(734) 998-0131

One of the great features about Ann Arbor beside it being a college town and the home of the Wolverines is that everything is within walking distance. When I first moved to Ann Arbor, I didn't have a car. Ali Baba's was only a five minute walk from my apartment. Thank goodness it was so tasty, because I must have eaten there three times a week! Ali Baba's offers Lebanese cuisine at affordable prices. Their specialties include chicken shawarma, fattoush, falafel, baba ghanouj and lentil soup.

ARBOR BREWING COMPANY
Eberwhite

114 East Washington St.
Ann Arbor, MI 48104

(734) 213-1393 | www.arborbrewing.com

Great food, service and a smoke-free environment makes for a great start. The Arbor Brewing Company is known for its award-winning beer. Be the dad who goes there for the food. They serve American cuisine.

ARGIERO'S ITALIAN RESTAURANT
Eberwhite

300 Detroit St.
Ann Arbor, MI 48104

(734) 665-1300 | www.argieros.net

When you're hungry for a taste of pure Italian, then you hunger for Argiero's Italian Restaurant. They serve an excellent variety of Italian dishes. Some say the best in town. However, a personal taste test is the best way to know. Be the dad who brings his children along on his quest for the best.

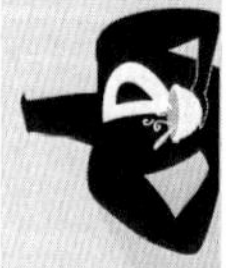

AYAKA
Eberwhite

1205 South University Ave.
Ann Arbor, MI 48104
(734) 214-1212

Being a university town, Ann Arbor is home to students and people from all over the world. The cuisines available in Ann Arbor reflect its diverse population. Ayaka offers authentic Japanese cuisine. The menu sports roughly fifty different varieties of regular sushi rolls. Their specialty rolls are the volcano, red dragon and fire crunch, as well as sushi/sashimi.

BANDITO'S
Eberwhite

216 South Fourth Ave.
Ann Arbor, MI 48104
(734) 996-0234

Ann Arbor is home to a lot of authentic restaurants. Bandito's is an authentic Mexican restaurant with its specialties being burritos, fajitas, quesadillas, and chimichangas. Be the dad who knows where to get mouth-watering Mexican cuisine.

BAR LOUIE
Eberwhite

401 East Liberty St.
Ann Arbor, MI 48104
(734) 794 3000 | www.restaurants-america.com

Bar Louie's may not be your dinner destination every night of the week with your children, but don't rule out special occasions. The ambience and the food will be a fine dinning experience. Be the dad who knows where to have that special and memorable dinner.

BTB BURRITO
Eberwhite

810 South State St.
Ann Arbor, MI 48104
(734) 222-4922 | www.btbburrito.com

BTB Burrito is the place to go for economically priced burritos, tacos and quesadillas. When you need a lot and you need it quick, BTB is the place to go. Be the dad who knows how to save and budget.

CAFÉ FELIX
Eberwhite

204 South Main St.
Ann Arbor, MI 48104
(734) 662-8650 | www.cafefelix.com

Café Felix opened its doors in 1997 and was primarily a coffeehouse. In 1999, they served their first glass of wine and a tradition was born. Their house specialties are seafood, exotic salads, thin-crust pizza, gourmet sandwiches and desserts. Be the dad who knows where to go for that very special occasion.

CAFÉ HABANA
Eberwhite

211 East Washington St.
Ann Arbor, MI 48104

(734) 332-6046 | www.cafehabana.com

Café Habana is the perfect destination for Cuban and Latin cuisine. Café Habana is located in the heart of downtown Ann Arbor. WonderDads add Cuban and Latin cuisine to their children's culinary education.

CAKE NOUVEAU
Eberwhite

1924 Packard St.
Ann Arbor, MI 48104

(734) 994-4033 | www.cafenoueau.com

Cake Nouveau is the place to go to satisfy that sweet tooth most children seem to have. Nouveau serves four rotating flavors of cupcakes daily. They also sell cake by the slice. Be the dad who knows where to get the cake and let them eat it, too.

CAFÉ VERDE
Eberwhite

216 North Fourth Ave.
Ann Arbor, MI 48104

(734) 302-7032 | www.peoplesfood.coop

Café Verde is a grocery store with a deli inside. They are known for serving fair-trade organic coffees, home-baked pastries, and having a "Fabulous Food Bar." They serve daily hot entrées, three soups daily, fresh salad, and deli takeout foods. Be the dad who knows organic foods are both healthy and good for you.

CAFÉ ZOLA
Eberwhite

112 West Washington St.
Ann Arbor, MI 48104

(734) 769-2020 | www.cafezola.com

The words bistro and breakfast go well together, especially at Café Zola. Zola's opened its doors in 1996 and quickly became a favorite breakfast, lunch, and dinner destination. The menus at Zola's are mostly inspired by French cuisines. Be the hero who lets Mom sleep in on Saturday morning by taking the children for a weekend brunch at Zola's.

CASEY'S TAVERN
Eberwhite

304 Depot St.
Ann Arbor, MI 48104

(734) 665-6775

Casey's Tavern is a classic neighborhood restaurant which serves a nice selection of sandwiches and burgers. Be the dad who knows children like to eat burgers and fries.

CHAMPION HOUSE RESTAURANT
Eberwhite

120 East Liberty St.
Ann Arbor, MI 48104
(734) 741-8100

I remember when I was growing up going to Benihana for dinner with my parents. It was an exciting and tasty evening. The Champion House Restaurant offers that same tasty excitement in Ann Arbor. You can choose your meal and then watch the chef prepare it right before your eyes. Champion House is known for its Japanese cuisine and sushi bar. Be the dad who creates a lifelong tasty memory.

CLOVERLEAF RESTAURANT
Eberwhite

201 East Liberty St.
Ann Arbor, MI 48104
(734) 662-1266

Cloverleaf Restaurant has been a downtown family diner in the Ann Arbor community for 35 years. They offer many breakfast specialties along with serving lunch and dinner.

CONOR O'NEILL'S TRADITIONAL IRISH PUB & RESTAURANT
Eberwhite

318 South Main St.
Ann Arbor, MI 48104
(734) 665-2968 | www.conoroneils.com

Growing up, we had a family tradition of going to an Irish pub on New Year's Eve to celebrate. We sang traditional Irish songs, had dinner, and counted down the New Year. I had many a fine meal, no alcohol, and lots of fond memories. Conor O'Neil's is an authentic Irish pub.

EARTHEN JAR
Eberwhite

311 South Fifth Ave.
Ann Arbor, MI 48104
(734) 327-9464 | www.earthenjar.com

The Earthen Jar is a vegetable lover's paradise. The Jar features Vegan cuisine with a North Indian style of cooking. Their featured buffet is a $5.99, mostly Vegan spread. Be the dad who promotes a healthy lifestyle fueled with healthy eating habits.

EASTERN ACCENTS

Eberwhite

214 South Fourth Ave.
Ann Arbor, MI 48104
(734) 332-8782

There's something about fresh-baked pastries that's warm and inviting. Eastern Accents is a pan-Asian bakery. They offer both sweet and savory pastries. Be the dad who knows a good pastry when he tastes one. Eastern Accents also serves a light lunch as well as many specialty items.

EVE - THE RESTAURANT

Eberwhite

415 North Fifth Ave.
Ann Arbor, MI 48104
(734) 222-0711

Eve—The Restaurant is an excellent example of the ambience and fare offered at a Kerrytown restaurant. Eve's menu features contemporary French cuisine. However, you must be on your toes because the menu changes with the season and highlights locally grown produce. Be the dad who knows a good deal when he tastes it.

FLEETWOOD DINER

Eberwhite

300 South Ashley St.
Ann Arbor, MI 48104
(734) 995-5502

The Fleetwood Diner has become the go-to place of 24-hour diners in Ann Arbor. They serve an ample breakfast, lunch and dinner. Be the dad who understands what history, tradition and food have to do with one another.

JAMAICAN JERK PIT

Eberwhite

314 South Thayer St.
Ann Arbor, MI 48104
(734) 995-5375

Foods from the Caribbean have a very distinctive flavor. The Jamaican Jerk Pit features Jamaican jerk meats, vegetables, sandwiches and breads. Be the dad who brings home a taste of the tropics without a plane ticket.

JERUSALEM GARDEN

Eberwhite

307 South Fifth Ave.
Ann Arbor, MI 48104
(734) 995-5060 | www.jerusalemgarden.net

Jerusalem Garden opened its doors in 1987 and quickly became very well-known throughout the Ann Arbor area. Be the dad who knows where to get the best in Middle Eastern cuisine.

JOLLY PUMPKIN CAFE AND BREWERY

Eberwhite

311 South Main St.
Ann Arbor, MI 48104
(734) 913-2730 | www.jollypumpkin.com

The Jolly Pumpkin is Ann Arbor's newest brew-pub. Besides some very tantalizing brews, the menu has a nice selection of salads, sandwiches, pizzas and desserts. WonderDads will love the laid-back feeling, the kid-friendly menu, and the great brews.

KAI GARDEN

Eberwhite

116 South Main St.
Ann Arbor, MI 48104
(734) 995-1786

The Kai Garden offers new-line Chinese cuisine. Kai Garden is very well known for specializing in Hong Kong, Taiwanese, and Szechuan & Hunan style fare. Be the dad who knows were to get authentic Chinese cuisine.

KILWIN'S CHOCOLATES

Eberwhite

107 East Liberty St.
Ann Arbor, MI 48104
(734) 769-7759 | www.kilwins.com

Children, candy, and ice cream go hand-in-hand. All dads know the candy store is his best friend. Kilwin's is known for fine chocolates and its original-recipe ice cream.

KOSMOPOLITAN

Eberwhite

415 North Fifth Ave. - 1st Floor
Ann Arbor, MI 48104
(734) 668-4070 | www.kerrytown.com/kosmopolitan

Kosmopolitan is very well-known with the younger crowd who lives for their burgers, hand-cut fries, and grilled-cheese sandwiches. They also specialize in delicious Korean dishes like Bi-Bim Bop, Bulgogi, and Twigim. Be the dad who goes where it's been kid tested and approved.

LE DOG

Eberwhite

410 East Liberty St.
Ann Arbor, MI 48104
(734) 665-2114

In a college town, gourmet hot dogs and soups made from scratch are king. Le Dog is an Ann Arbor legend! They are also very affordable.

LOGAN AN AMERICAN RESTAURANT
Eberwhite

115 West Washington St.
Ann Arbor, MI 48104
(734) 327-2312 | www.logan-restaurant.com
Logan's offers what is called a New American cuisine with influences from Asia, Latin America and the Mediterranean.

MAHEK INDIAN CUISINE
Eberwhite

212 East Washington St.
Ann Arbor, MI 48104
(734) 994-5972 | www.mahekannarbor.com
The use of herbs and spices in certain cuisines dates back several centuries. Mahek's is a fine example of centuries-old, authentic Indian food. Be the dad who brings home the original stuff.

MÉLANGE BISTRO & WINE BAR
Eberwhite

314 South Main St.
Ann Arbor, MI 48104
(734) 222-0202 | www.melangebistro.com
Mélange offers a menu that blends European and Asian cuisines. The eclectic cuisines are infused with worldly ingredients, while the aesthetically pleasing atmosphere creates a special ambience that can only be experienced in person. Be the dad who takes advantage of this experience.

MERCY'S AT THE BELL TOWER
Eberwhite

300 South Thayer St.
Ann Arbor, MI 48104
(734) 994-0222 | www.belltowerhotel.com
The Bell Tower hotel is home to a French and Indian restaurant called Mercy's. The menu offers delectable gourmet entrées such as coriander-dusted sea scallops, rack of lamb de Provence, and Maughinga. Be the dad who brings in culture and a fine dinning experience to his son/daughter relationship.

MIDDLE KINGDOM
Eberwhite

332 South Main St.
Ann Arbor, MI 48104
(734) 668-6638
Middle Kingdom offers a unique blend of Caribbean, Mandarin, Cantonese, and Szechuan cuisines. Be the dad who brings a little bit of everything home by going to one restaurant.

MONAHAN'S SEAFOOD MARKET
Eberwhite

407 North Fifth Ave.
Ann Arbor, MI 48104
(734) 662-5118 | www.kerrytown.com/monahans

Monahan's Seafood Market is a seafood lover's dream. They sell an awesome selection of fresh or smoked fish, shellfish, and appetizers. Be the dad who snacks on a little soft-shell crab for lunch with his son or daughter.

OLD TOWN TAVERN
Eberwhite

122 West Liberty St.
Ann Arbor, MI 48104
(734) 662-9291 | www.oldtownaa.com

The Old Town Tavern offers a relaxed ambience that makes it easy to enjoy good food. They claim to have the best burger in town. However, I believe a taste test is required. Be the dad who brings his kids in as guest judges.

PACIFIC RIM
Eberwhite

114 West Liberty St.
Ann Arbor, MI 48104
(734) 662-9303 | www.pacificrimbykana.com

Pacific Rim offers the finest in pan-Asian cuisine. The Rim specializes in providing interesting sauces to go on its fresh fish and seafood. They also offer exotic and unusual appetizers, like Unagi Terrine, broiled eel with avocado and sushi rice served with a soy syrup and wasabi oil.

PARTHENON RESTAURANT
Eberwhite

226 South Main St.
Ann Arbor, MI 48104
(734) 994-1012 | www.parthenonrestaurant.net

The Parthenon Restaurant serves a delicious array of Greek and Italian cuisine. Be the dad who knows were to find the tastes of the old world.

RAJA RANI RESTAURANT
Eberwhite

400 South Division St.
Ann Arbor, MI 48104
(734) 995-1545

There's something to be said for being first. Raja Rani is Michigan's oldest family-owned and operated Indian restaurant. Be the dad who supports family values.

SABOR LATINO RESTAURANT
Eberwhite

211 North Main St.
Ann Arbor, MI 48104
(734) 214-7775

Sabor Latino offers authentic cuisines from all over Latin America. Be the dad who does a South American taste tour all in one afternoon.

SIAM CUISINE THAI RESTAURANT
Eberwhite

313 North Fourth Ave.
Ann Arbor, MI 48104
(734) 663-4083 | www.siam-cuisine.com

If you are looking for authentic, then look no further than Siam's for authentic Thai cuisines. Siam's menu selection offers a wide range of dishes, starting with mild and on up to very spicy. Be the dad who adds a little spice to his child's life.

SOTTINI'S SUB SHOP
Eberwhite

205 South Fourth Ave.
Ann Arbor, MI 48104
(734) 769-7827

When nothing but a submarine sandwich will do, go to Sottini's Sub Shop. Sottini's is located in the heart of downtown Ann Arbor and has a variety of delicious menu items to choose from. WonderDads know where to grab lunch on the go.

SQUARES RESTAURANT
Eberwhite

241 East Liberty St.
Ann Arbor, MI 48104
(734) 761-6700 | www.annarbor.squaresrestaurant.com

Squares would be the place for breakfast or a quick lunch. They offer omelets, salads and sandwiches made on their signature square bread. They also have a wide assortment of smoothies. This is the perfect location for a Saturday afternoon son or daughter lunch date.

SWEETWATER'S CAFÉ
Eberwhite

123 West Washington St.
Ann Arbor, MI 48104
(734) 769-2331 | www.sweetwaterscafe.com

While visiting downtown Ann Arbor, stop by Sweetwater's for a cup of coffee or an espresso; meanwhile, your children can enjoy a frozen ice dragon, desserts or pastries. They also have Wi-Fi capabilities. Oh...be sure to say hi to the fairies.

SWIRLBERRY
Eberwhite

209 South State St.
Ann Arbor, MI 48104
(734) 222-1707 | www.swirlberry.com

Swirlberry serves a tangy fat- and gluten-free frozen yogurt with lots of healthy bacteria in several unique flavors. Be the dad who knows where to get a tasty and healthy afternoon treat.

THE ARENA
Eberwhite

203 East Washington St.
Ann Arbor, MI 48104
(734) 222-9999

The Arena is considered Ann Arbor's premier sports bar. Be the dad who kills two birds with one stone. The sports bar serves an all-American cuisine, has twenty-four draughts on tap, four HD big-screen televisions and twenty-two satellite televisions. The sports bar is also child- and family-friendly.

THE BLACK PEARL
Eberwhite

302 South Main St.
Ann Arbor, MI 48104
(734) 222-0400 | www.theblackpearlonmain.com

Ann Arbor has a thriving restaurant community. The Black Pearl is a new addition to the restaurant scene offering a seafood and martini bar. Be the dad who visits for dinner and stays for the live entertainment.

THE BLUE LEPRECHAUN
Eberwhite

1220 South University Ave.
Ann Arbor, MI 48104
(734) 665-7777 | www.theblueleprechaun.com

The Blue Leprechaun offers a blend of American and Irish lip-smacking cuisines. They also have a few big-screen plasma televisions. This is the perfect venue for dad to watch the big game, feed the children and educate their paletes all in one fell swoop. Well, maybe not watch the game as much as get a sneak peek at the big game. In any event, the Blue Leprechaun offers authentic Irish cuisine.

THE BROKEN EGG
Eberwhite

223 North Main St.
Ann Arbor, MI 48104
(734) 665-5340

The Broken Egg offers what its name sake suggests. You can get a delicious, full breakfast or lunch. Their home-style soups and salads are also a big hit. Be the dad who delivers on a home-cooked breakfast without waking mom on the weekend.

THE CHOP HOUSE
Eberwhite

322 South Main St.
Ann Arbor, MI 48104

(734) 669-8826 | www.thechophouserestaurant.com

The Chop House features a delectable array of delicious, prime grain-fed meats with an exceptional list of wines to go with the meal. Be the dad who knows where to feed his meat-and-potato-eating children.

THE CUPCAKE STATION
Eberwhite

120 East Liberty St.
Ann Arbor, MI 48104

(734) 222-1801 | www.cupcakestation.com

Cupcakes are big business in Ann Arbor. The Cupcake Station offers a nice selection of fresh-baked cupcakes. Cupcakes are a delicious and economical dessert alternative. Be the dad who saves money and delivers the goods at the same time.

THE MELTING POT
Eberwhite

309 South Main St.
Ann Arbor, MI 48104

(734) 622-0055 | www.themeltingpot.com

Everything is better dipped in chocolate. The Melting Pot is consider one of Ann Arbor's premier dating restaurants, but family get-togethers or birthday parties would be a fun experience as well. Be the dad who mixes chocolate, fondue and family fun.

THE ORIGINAL COTTAGE INN
Eberwhite

512 East William St.
Ann Arbor, MI 48104

(734) 663-3379 | www.cottageinn.com

The Cottage Inn franchise can boast it has Ann Arbor's first pizzeria. Be the dad who brings home a little history and a great-tasting dinner.

TIAN CHU KOREAN RESTAURANT
Eberwhite

613 East William St.
Ann Arbor, MI 48104

(734) 769-1368

Ann Arbor is home to a wide range of international students. Tian Chu opened her Korean restaurant in 2010 near the Eastern Michigan campus. The restaurant offers a delicious selection of Korean, Chinese, and Japanese cuisines. Korean food is simple, fresh and tasty, and many dishes are fairly plain. Add it to your repertoire and pretty soon you'll never be out of options when nobody wants to cook. Plus, you'll help your kids learn to try new things.

TK WU

Eberwhite

510 East Liberty St.
Ann Arbor, MI 48104
(734) 747-6662 | www.tkwu.com

The TK Wu restaurant opened its doors in 2003 and is named after the owner/chef's two children Tiffany and Kevin. The restaurant serves authentic Chinese and Asian cuisine.

TOTORO

Eberwhite

215 South State St.
Ann Arbor, MI 48104
(734) 302-3511 | www.totoroannarbor.com

Raw fish prepared correctly is healthy for you. Totoro's is on the campus of the University of Michigan and offers authentic Japanese cuisine. Be the dad who leads the way in trying new things.

WASHTENAW DAIRY

Eberwhite

602 South Ashley St.
Ann Arbor, MI 48104
(734) 662-3244 | www.washtenawdairy.com

The Washtenaw Dairy is an Ann Arbor institution. They have been delivering quality dairy products since 1931. The dairy offers 30 varieties of ice creams and donuts made from scratch. Be the dad who knows how to bring home the good stuff.

WEST END GRILL

Eberwhite

120 West Liberty St.
Ann Arbor, MI 48104
(734) 747-6260

The West End Grill is an exciting new dining option. Their menu is what is considered New American cuisine with a flair. They plate up fresh seafood and steaks with an Asian influence.

NORTHSIDE GRILL

King & Logan

1015 Broadway St.
Ann Arbor, MI 48105
(734) 995-0965

Eating down-home food is a good thing. When it's affordable, it's even better. The Northside Grill serves good food.

SAICA RESTAURANT
Northside & Thurston

1733 Plymouth Rd.
Ann Arbor, MI 48105
(734) 769-1212
www.menuism.com/restaurants/sacia-restaurants-annarbor
Saica serves Asian and Japanese cuisines. They are particularly known for the sushi and affordable prices. One review termed the cuisine as Japanese comfort food.

ANTHONY'S GOURMET PIZZA
Abbot/Haisley/Wines

1508 North Maple St.
Ann Arbor, MI 48103
(734) 213-2500 | www.anthonysgourmetpizza.com
Anthony's Gourmet Pizza is an excellent dining option. They offer handmade deep-dish and Chicago-style stuffed pizza with a wide range of toppings that make it well worth the price. The menu also includes subs, calzones and flatbreads as appetizers. Be the dad who brings home a gourmet pizza.

BRAZAMERICA
Abbot/Haisley/Wines

619 South Main St.
Ann Arbor, MI 48104
(734) 996-0123 | www.brazamerica.com
Shopping at Brazamerica allows you to bring the taste of Brazil home. Be the dad who helps to broaden his child's palette and mind at the same time.

CAFÉ JAPON JAPANESE RESTAURANT
Abbot/Haisley/Wines

113 East Liberty St.
Ann Arbor, MI 48104
(734) 332-6200 | www.cafejapon.net
Café Japon offers authentic Japanese and French cuisines with the slogan "slow food for busy people." They are known for great French pastries and health-conscious gourmet meals. They also have a full selection of exotic teas. This is the perfect way for a hero to introduce healthy cuisine into his child's diet.

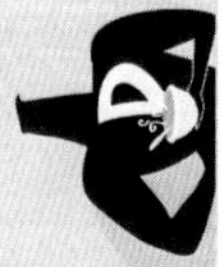

CARIBOU COFFEE
Abbot/Haisley/Wines

1423 East Stadium Blvd. #A
Ann Arbor, MI 48104
(734) 222-0205 | www.cariboucoffee.com

Coffee shops have always held a special significance for me. Among the many special things I got to share with my father, coffee was one of them. I was a coffee drinker early in life and this love affair with coffee has grown into a daily habit. In some way, the quaint, cozy, and intimate atmosphere always reminds me of a special time shared. Caribou Coffee has the ambience of just such a place. The unique flavors of coffee aren't bad either. Be the dad who finds ways to share a special time with his son or daughter.

LA DOLCE VITA
Abbot/Haisley/Wines

322 South Main St.
Ann Arbor, MI 48104
(734) 669-9977

La Dolce Vita is an ideal place to go for a romantic dessert date. The specialties of the house are baked goods, desserts and coffee. Every WonderDad deserves a night out with his lady.

LITTLE PORKY'S PIZZA-N-MORE
Abbot/Haisley/Wines

2529 Dexter Rd.
Ann Arbor, MI 48103
(734) 213-2222 | www.allmenus.com

Little Porky's is known for having great soul food, particularly their Saint Louis ribs and fantastic pizzas. If you log on to www.allmenus.com, plug in restaurant or cuisino near Ann Arbor and Little Porky's full menu is available. Bringing home some good barbeque makes every dad a WonderDad for the night.

METZGER'S GERMAN RESTAURANT
Abbot/Haisley/Wines

305 North Zeeb Rd.
Ann Arbor, MI 48103
(734) 668-8987 | www.metzgers.net

Metzger's has been serving authentic German cuisine in Ann Arbor for more than 80 years. My personal favorites include Schnitzel and their full array of decadent desserts. Be the dad who broadens his child's horizons.

SAVA'S
Abbot/Haisley/Wines

216 South State St.
Ann Arbor, MI 48104
(734) 623-2233 | www.savasrestaurant.com

Sava's is new to Ann Arbor, opening its doors in 2007. The décor inside of the restaurant is warm and inviting. They serve a wide array of eclectic dishes that titillate the senses. Be the dad who shares the elegance of a night on the town with great ambience.

THE BLUE NILE
Abbot/Haisley/Wines

221 East Washington St.
Ann Arbor, MI 48104
(734) 998-4746 | www.bluenilemi.com

At the restaurant you sit around a low table on pillows. The food is served on a big platter and everyone eats from the same plate using their hands and torn flatbread to scoop up delicious stews. What kid doesn't want to eat with their hands?

THE BROWN JUG
Abbot/Haisley/Wines

1204 South University Ave.
Ann Arbor, MI 48104
(734) 761-3355 | www.brownjug-annarbor.com

The Brown Jug is an Ann Arbor tradition and has been so since opening its doors in 1938. During the day, they serve fabulous family-style cuisines and at night, well, it is a college town. If you decide to stop in, be sure to order Uncle Pat's Pizza.

OUTBACK STEAKHOUSE
Abbot/Haisley/Wines

3173 Oak Valley Dr.
Ann Arbor, MI 48103
(734) 662-7400 | www.outback.com

Taking that meat eater in the family to Outback Steakhouse is a sure winner. The specialty of the house is their steak and lobster tail meal followed by a wide array of other menu selections. In addition to their regular menu, Outback offers a gluten-free menu.

UPTOWN CONEY ISLAND
Abbot/Haisley/Wines

3917 Jackson Rd.
Ann Arbor, MI 48103
(734) 665-5909 | www.uptownconey.com

Uptown Coney Island opened its doors in 1990 based on the theory of serving families a great meal at a reasonable price. Uptown is a very popular restaurant. If I were a dad with a family to feed, I would not leave Uptown Coney Island off my dining list. Uptown is known for having fabulous Greek cuisine.

AMADEUS CAFÉ & RESTAURANT

Allen & Bryant/Pattengill – East

122 East Washington St. #B
Ann Arbor, MI 48104

(734) 665-8767 | www.amadeusrestaurant.com

Amadeus offers a unique dining experience in a restaurant atmosphere fashioned after the old-world Viennese café. The restaurant cuisines are a mixture of Central Europe featuring fare from Poland, Hungary, and Austria. Amadeus opened its doors in 1988. This is another must-visit for that heroes' world tour.

BOB EVANS RESTAURANT

Allen & Bryant/Pattengill – East

2411 Carpenter Rd.
Ann Arbor, MI 48108

(734) 971-2220 | www.bobevans.com

Bob Evans is a family style restaurant which offers homemade meals like you were seated at the kitchen table at home. They say that breakfast is the most important meal of the day. While breakfast out may not be practical on a school morning, it sure is nice on the weekends.

CHUCK E CHEESE

Allen & Bryant/Pattengill – East

2655 Oak Valley Dr.
Ann Arbor, MI 48108

(734) 222-1003 | www.chuckecheese.com

I remember attending a birthday party for a friend's child at Chuck E. Cheese in Saginaw, Michigan. I also remember joking about the big rodent. But, I must confess the birthday girl completely enjoyed herself. It was a great place to have a child's birthday party. Every child in attendance had smiles on their faces all night long.

GREAT LAKE CHINESE SEAFOOD RESTAURANT

Allen & Bryant/Pattengill – East

2910 Carpenter Rd.
Ann Arbor, MI 48108

(734) 973-6666

This restaurant has authentic Chinese food, and should be on any heroes list of restaurants to share with their family. From simple, familiar chinese food dishes like broccoli beef to more complex seafood creations, this place will keep you and the kids happy and full for years to come.

HEIDELBERG RESTAURANT

Allen & Bryant/Pattengill – East

215 North Main St.
Ann Arbor, MI 48104
(734) 663-7758 | www.theheidelberg.com

The Heidelberg offers a great family dining experience. The main menu has a variety of delectable dishes and the children's menu (11 and under) starts at $3.99. The menu at the Heidelberg has what I would term as numerous Americanized dishes. Everything looks warm, inviting and delicious. Be the dad who knows where to save a little and have a great dining experience at the same time.

MAX AND ERMA'S

Allen & Bryant/Pattengill – East

4445 East Eisenhower St.
Ann Arbor, MI 48108
(734) 998-0505 | www.maxandermas.com

The food at Max and Erma's is delicious, and this Michigan-based chain has just enough going on in each restaurant to keep the kids amused, and the kids' menu has just enough choices to please the picky.

MIKI JAPANESE CUISINE & SUSHI BAR

Allen & Bryant/Pattengill – East

106 First St.
Ann Arbor, MI 48104
(734) 665-8226 | www.mikirestaurant.com

One common misconception is that no cooking is involved in authentic Japanese food. While a lot of dishes are raw, far from all of them are. Be the dad who educates his children and introduces them to a new world of culinary delights. The dishes at Miki's are colorful and masterfully designed by authentic Japanese chefs. Don't be the hero who forgets to add this restaurant to the world tour.

RED ROBIN GOURMET BURGERS

Allen & Bryant/Pattengill – East

575 Briarwood Cir.
Ann Arbor, MI 48108
(734) 997-9550 | www.redrobin.com

The Red Robin Gourmet burger chain started in 1969 and now has over 450 locations nationwide. They are also known for having more than insanely delicious burgers. They sponsor a kids' cook-off where children from all over the country compete to create the ultimate burger and recipe. The competition is in its fifth year. The kids' cook-off cookbook offers 50 recipes from competitors all over the country. It can be downloaded free.

ROMANO'S MACARONI GRILL

Allen & Bryant/Pattengill – East

3010 South State St.
Ann Arbor, MI 48108
(734) 663-4433 | www.macaronigrill.com

Romano's offers over 35 authentic Italian dishes, including pastas, steaks, chicken, seafood, veal, and pizzas.

SAIGON GARDEN

Allen & Bryant/Pattengill – East

1220 South University Ave. #110
Ann Arbor, MI 48104
(734) 747-7006

No heroes' world tour would be complete without a chance to try Vietnamese cuisine. The Vietnamese food is authentic and tasty. Be the dad who adds Vietnamese cuisines to his child's bucket list.

SIAM SQUARE

Allen & Bryant/Pattengill – East

3750 Washtenaw Ave.
Ann Arbor, MI 48104
(734) 975-4541 | www.siamsquare.us/index.htm

Serving up authentic Thai dishes, including mild curries and jasmine rice. The grilled chicken skewers called satay are good choices for young kids who aren't familiar with more complex tastes.

THE EARLE

Allen & Bryant/Pattengill – East

121 West Washington St.
Ann Arbor, MI 48104
(734) 994-0211 | www.theearle.com

An evening at the Earle offers the best in French and Italian country cuisine, live music and the ambience of a fine dining establishment. Be the dad who brings fine dining and great memories.

WHITE CASTLE

Burns Park – East & Carpenter

3953 Packard St.
Ann Arbor, MI 48108
(734) 973-6811 | www.whitecastle.com

White Castle has a rich and storied history, laying claim to several business first. They were the first to sell one million hamburgers, first to sell one billion and the first to sell frozen fast food. White Castle first opened its doors in 1921. Be the dad who establishes great lifelong memories.

OLIVE GARDEN

Burns Park–East & Carpenter

445 East Eisenhower Pkwy.
Ann Arbor, MI 48108
(734) 663-6875 | www.olivegarden.com

For me, Olive Garden has been the restaurant of choice when I was actively dating and still holds that ambience now that I'm married. If you like authentic Italian cuisine, then this is your restaurant. Be the dad who creates lasting delicious memories with his son or daughter.

MADRAS MASALA

Mitchell & Pittsfield

328 Maynard St.
Ann Arbor, MI 48104
(734) 222-9006 | www.madrasmasala.com

Madras Masala serves authentic Indian cuisine. They also have a terrific takeout menu complete with dishes to make the Vegan in all of us happy. This restaurant is a must for the hero and his children making the world tour.

ANGELO'S RESTAURANT

Bryan/Pattengill–West/
Dicken/Lakewood/Lawton

100 Catherine St.
Ann Arbor, MI 48104
(734) 761-8996 | www.angelosa2.com

Angelo's is an Ann Arbor tradition which started in 1956. The business was originally run by Angelo Vangelatos and his wife, Patricia. In 1986 Angelo retired and his son, Steve, and his wife Jenifer took over the family business. Be the dad who adds family tradition and great food to the mix. Angelo's is known for its on-site bakery and coffee house.

GRANGE KITCHEN & BAR

Bryan/Pattengill–West/
Dicken/Lakewood/Lawton

118 West Liberty St.
Ann Arbor, MI 48104
(734) 995-2107 | www.grangekitchenandbar.com

Grange's is your local source for farm-to-table dining. The restaurant's specialties are Italian and French cuisines that focus on bringing in the best local produce available and serving it at its peak of flavor. This is also a very healthy way to eat. Be the dad who knows where to get fresh healthy cuisine.

GRIZZLY PEAK BREWING COMPANY

Bryan/Pattengill – West/ Dicken/Lakewood/Lawton

120 Washington St.
Ann Arbor, MI 48104

(734) 741-7325 | www.grizzlypeak.net

Grizzly Peak's is a unique and special restaurant that first opened its doors in 1995 and quickly became an Ann Arbor favorite. The restaurant was established in a century-old building with wood floors and exposed brick walls which all add up to a terrific dining environment. One of the unique features of the restaurant is the seven-barrel on-site brewery. Patrons can view the brew being made.

KNIGHT'S STEAK HOUSE

Bryan/Pattengill – West/ Dicken/Lakewood/Lawton

2324 Dexter Ave.
Ann Arbor, MI 48103

(734) 665-8644 | www.knightsrestaurant.com

Knight's Steak House is a family owned restaurant which opened its doors in 1984. They offer a selection of meat cut daily, an on-site bakery and daily home-made soups. The prices are affordable and the food is excellent. A dad couldn't go wrong bringing his family to dine at Knight's Steak House.

MAIZE N BLUE DELICATESSEN

Bryan/Pattengill – West/ Dicken/Lakewood/Lawton

1329 South University Ave. #A
Ann Arbor, MI 48104

(734) 996-0009

The Maize N Blue Delicatessen has a terrific selection of sandwiches. But, with a name like Maize N Blue in the heart of a college football crazy town—what would you expect. The food is also very good. Be the dad who completes the Michigan football experience by dining at the Maize N Blue before watching the Maize and Blue live.

THE BEST DAD/CHILD
ACTIVITIES

ANN ARBOR ART CENTER

Angell

117 West Liberty St.
Ann Arbor, MI 48104

(734) 994-8004 | www.annarborartcenter.org

Be the hero who helps your child travel back in time by visiting an Ann Arbor landmark. The Art Center was established in 1909 and features three main galleries. The Art Center caters to families with fabulous year-round opportunities for hands-on, kid-friendly art instruction and appreciation classes.

KEMPF HOUSE MUSEUM

Angell

312 South Division St.
Ann Arbor, MI 48104

(734) 994-4898

Have you ever participated in a German Christmas? Well, a visit to the Kempf House Museum will help make that possible. The museum is a restored 19th-century Greek revival home.

KINDLE FEST

Angell

Kerrytown Market and Shops
315 Detroit St.
Ann Arbor, MI 48104

(734) 794-6255

Be the dad who exposes your child to a little culture. The Kindle Fest Market offers a taste of Europe with its artisans, farmers and retailers selling their holiday wares, which include traditional foods, mulled wine, and beer.

LYDIA MENDELSSOHN THEATRE

Angell

911 North University Ave.
Ann Arbor, MI 48104

(734) 764-2538

Be the cool guy who knows about Salsa. Baby Loves Salsa is a one hour family performance. José Conde, well known as the leader of the New York-based band Ola Fresca, presents an Afro-Cuban form of salsa, which he turns into something special that kids and parents will love. Cost: $16 adults, $8 children.

MAIN ST. ICE CARVING EXTRAVAGANZA

Angell

Downtown
Ann Arbor, MI 48104

Get the kids front-row seats when blocks of ice become one-of-a-kind works of art, and they'll never forget it. The University of Michigan Ice Carving Team will create commissioned sculptures on the sidewalks of Main St., Liberty St., Washington St., and Fourth Ave.

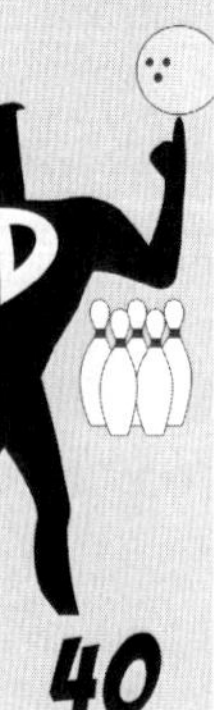

PINBALL PETE'S
Angell

1214 South University Ave.
Ann Arbor, MI 48104
(734) 213-2502

I remember growing up in Norwich, Connecticut, and almost not being able to wait until Saturday afternoon so I could go to the arcade. It was good, clean, economical fun. A place my allowance could afford. Be the dad who knows what a great arcade means to his kids.

ANN ARBOR DISTRICT LIBRARY
Bach

343 South Fifth Ave.
Ann Arbor, MI 48104
(734) 327-4200

The public library is a great resource for all heroes or dads. In particular the downtown branch offers a program called "Stories to Go." This service is an excellent resource for dads because it offers a selection of materials for young children organized around a theme. The kits include a selection of picture books on the theme, CDs or DVDs relating to the theme, and a resource folder containing a list of games and activities related to the theme. There is a wide range of kits available on numerous, relevant themes. This is an excellent resource for all dads and well worth your time and effort.

NICHOLS ARBORETUM
Bach

1610 Washington Heights
Ann Arbor, MI 48104
(734) 647-7600 | www.lsa.umich.edu

Be the hero that helps expand his child's knowledge base by visiting the Nichols Arboretum, which is home to hundreds of species of plants native to Michigan. There is no cost to visit and it's open Monday through Sunday from 8a.m. until dusk.

BURNS PARK CENTRAL
Bach

Sunday Artisan Market
315 Detroit St.
Ann Arbor, MI 48104
(734) 913-9622

The Artisan Market is open every Sunday from May through November. The market is an open-air market that offers handmade items and unique, creative gifts from local Ann Arbor vendors. Be the dad who knows where to find unique, one-of-a-kind handmade gifts.

BALLET THEATRE
Eberwhite

The Power Center
121 Fletcher St.
Ann Arbor, MI 48104
(734) 763-3333

All cool dads have a little culture in their repertoire. The Ann Arbor Ballet Theatre presents "The Nutcracker." Cost: adults - $24; students & seniors: $20; children under 12: $14 Friday and Saturday at 8p.m.; Saturday and Sunday at 2p.m.

WASHTENAW COUNTY WAR MEMORIAL
Eberwhite

1399 Geddes Ave.
Ann Arbor, MI 48104

The Civil War was America's bloodiest incursion on American soil, which brought an end to slavery. This memorial was erected in 1914 to honor the soldiers of Washtenaw County who fought in the Civil War (1861-1865) and the war in Spain (1898). Be the WonderDad who shows his kids what real heroism looks like.

DOMINO'S PETTING FARM
King & Logan

24 Frank Lloyd Wright Dr.
Ann Arbor, MI 48105
(734) 998-0182 | www.pettingfarm.com

I couldn't believe my eyes when I saw a live buffalo up close. Talk about reaching out and experiencing a bit of history. This Petting Farm is a combination farm and zoo, which houses more than 100 animals, including many rare breeds. Be the hero who takes his child on their first pony or hayride. The farm is open Monday-Friday from 9:30-4pm, but closed New Year's, Thanksgiving & Christmas.

EXHIBIT MUSEUM OF NATURAL HISTORY
King & Logan

1109 Geddes Ave
Ann Arbor, MI 48109-1079
(734) 764-0480 | www.lsa.umich/exhibitmuseum

Be the hero that sparks his child's imagination and love for history. The museum's permanent exhibits include dinosaurs and other prehistoric life, Michigan wildlife, Native-American culture, anthropology, geology, and a planetarium. There is no cost to visit Monday-Saturday from 9-5p.m. and Sun from noon until 5p.m. with suggested donations of $6 for adults and $3 for children.

ID TECH CAMPS
King & Logan

University of Michigan
Ann Arbor, MI 48109
(888) 709-8324 | www.internaldrive.com

ID Tech Camp is an elite computer camp offered at the University of Michigan and is considered one of the top computer camps in the country. The camp is designed for beginners to advanced learners. The day camp and overnight camp classes average six students per instructor and the curriculum offers the latest in cutting-edge computer software and technology. Be the dad who adds computer learning power to his son or daughter's repertoire.

JEAN PAUL SLUSSER GALLERY
King & Logan

2000 Bonisteel Blvd.
Ann Arbor, MI 48109
(734) 936-2982 | www.michigan.org

Viewing the works of art at the Slusser Gallery is a unique cultural experience. All of the artwork in the gallery is done by students and faculty from the University of Michigan School of Art and Design and the School of Architecture. Log on to www.michigan.org and type in Slusser Gallery for more information.

MARGARET DOW TOWSLEY SPORTS MUSEUM
King & Logan

1200 South State St.
Ann Arbor, MI 48109
(734) 747-2583 | www.hvcn.org

If you are a Michigan fan and you want your children's first words to be "Go Blue," then this is the place to be. This museum displays exclusively Michigan athletics memorabilia. It covers all 25 sports and is complete with touch-screen TVs, mini videos, and display cases. The museum is located in Schembechler Hall.

RACKHAM AUDITORIUM
King & Logan

915 East Washington St.
Ann Arbor, MI 48109
(734) 763-3333 | www.music.umich.edu

Ann Arbor is a college town that is full of cultural and musical opportunities. The Rackham Auditorium was built in the late 1930s by architect William Knapp and architectural sculptor Corrado Parducci. The facility soon became known as the place with the perfect acoustical pitch. Be the dad who introduces music into the lives of his children in the way it should be heard.

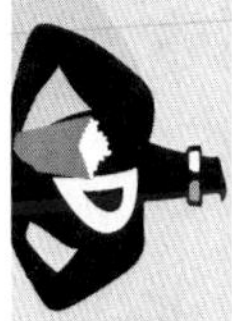

WASHTENAW COMMUNITY COLLEGE

King & Logan

Towsley Auditorium
4800 East Huron River Dr.
Ann Arbor, MI 48105
(734) 995-0530

Towsley Auditorium plays host to four plays geared specifically to young children. In the play Firebird, young Ivan, prince of Russia, must outwit numerous evil characters in his quest to find the Firebird, who has been stealing the Czar's golden apples. The play brings to life fantastical creatures, which include the witch Baba Yaga, Nurl the Gnome, and Sistchik the Snake King. Cost: $10–children $8-season tickets, $15–Adults, $12–season tickets. The adventures of Winnie the Pooh are acted out on stage. Children ages 3-9 will delight in joining Pooh as he hums his way through the Hundred Acre Woods or pretends to hunt heffalumps with Piglet. Cost: $10-children $8-season tickets, $15–Adults, $12–season tickets. Under the African Sky is a delightful and whimsical collection of African tales brought to life through storytelling, acting, and drumming. The play is complete with colorful costumes, masks, and traditional music. There is lots of audience participation as the play is geared toward children age 4-10. Cost: $10–children $8–season tickets, $15-Adults, $12-season ticket. The Adventures of Peter Rabbit are brought to life when Peter romps through Farmer McGregor's garden, despite his mother's warning. The play is geared for children age 3-9. Cost: $10–children $8–season tickets, $15–Adults, $12–season tickets.

LESLIE SCIENCE & NATURE CENTER

Northside & Thurston

1831 Traver Rd.
Ann Arbor, MI 48105
(734) 997-1553 | ci.ann.arbor.mi.us

Enter a magical world where flowers dance in the sunshine and children can pretend to hop with insects as they discover the world of tall grass. Cost: $7 per child per program. Concerned about our planet? Well, your child's education starts early. Children are taught what they can do to help care for the earth through songs, songwriting, fun outdoor experiences and environmentally themed games. Cost: $8/person.

CONCORDIA UNIVERSITY

Northside & Thurston

Chapel of the Holy Trinity
4090 Geddes Rd.
Ann Arbor, MI 48105
(734) 995-4612

The Boar's Head Festival has become an Ann Arbor tradition. The students, faculty and staff of Concordia University in Ann Arbor join forces to re-enact medieval Christmas traditions and the story of Christ's birth with a complete musical narration, congregational singing and a full orchestra. Cost is $8-$15.

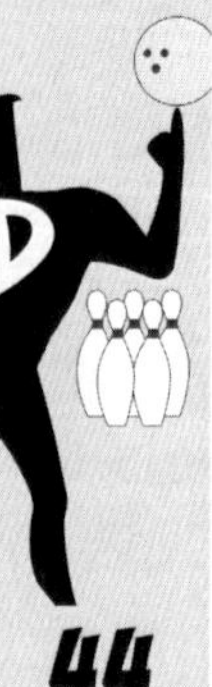

MATTHAEI BOTANICAL GARDENS

Northside & Thurston

1800 North Dixboro Rd.
Ann Arbor, MI 48105
(734) 647-7600

The beautiful and peaceful grounds are just the tip of the iceberg when you visit the botanical gardens. The 300-acre garden has a number of outdoor displays as well as tables and chairs for up to 100 people. Additionally, you can bring in your own food.

ACTIVE GIRL PROGRAM AT THE YMCA

Abbot/Haisley/Wines

400 West Washington St.
Ann Arbor, MI 48103
(734) 996-9622

The YMCA's active girl program is geared towards ages 6-9 years old. The program offers terrific opportunities for your young one to experience the benefits of physical activities in a safe, secure and supportive environment.

AIKIDO AT THE YMCA

Abbot/Haisley/Wines

400 West Washington St.
Ann Arbor, MI 48103
(734) 996-9622

The Y offers classes in Aikido for ages starting at 6 and up. Aikido is a martial art developed from the code of the Japanese samurai. The basic movements learned are based on fighting techniques which utilize balance, timing and alignment. The self-esteem and discipline developed in martial arts are wonderful tools to help your kids cultivate.

BASKETBALL AT THE YMCA

Abbot/Haisley/Wines

400 West Washington St.
Ann Arbor, MI 48103
(734) 966-9622

Be the dad who starts your child on their way to an athletic future. The YMCA has an awesome youth basketball clinic taught by experienced coaches who can help develop their motor skills through praise, encouragement and reinforcement. In addition, this is a great place for your child to make new friends and form life-long bonds. This basketball program is geared toward ages 5 and up.

EARLY CHILDHOOD PROGRAM AT THE YMCA
Abbot/Haisley/Wines

400 West Washington St.
Ann Arbor, MI 48103
(734) 996-9622

The YMCA is also the place to take children starting age 2 ½ to 3 ½ years old. The YMCA's full-day nationally accredited Early Childhood Program focuses on building strong children. The program guides children through an age-appropriate curriculum which develop self-help skills and instills the values of caring, honesty, respect and responsibility.

FARMERS' MARKET PAVILION
Abbot/Haisley/Wines

315 Detroit St.
Ann Arbor, MI 48104
(734) 794-6244

Located in the historic Kerrytown District in a lovely open-air marketplace, the Ann Arbor Farmers' Market features locally grown food, plants, handcrafts and prepared food items. The Ann Arbor Farmers' Market is a producers-only market, which means that all items for sale are grown, baked or crafted by the vendors who sell them.

FUNIFACES FACE PAINTING
Abbot/Haisley/Wines

(734) 915-1853 | www.funifaces.com

Just imagine having your mask painted on your face. Funifaces is an Ann Arbor based company which offers face painting. Be the dad who delivers with a unique and wonderful addition to any child's party. Funifaces can be contacted through email (funifaces@aol.com) or by phone.

JUDO AT THE YMCA
Abbot/Haisley/Wines

400 West Washington St.
Ann Arbor, MI 48103
(734) 996-9622

Judo classes at the Y are a great way to channel the pent up energy in your 8 year old into something productive and healthy. The techniques of self-defense in Judo are particularly useful for the undersized. It is the great equalizer. The YMCA Judo classes are for ages seven and up.

KARATE AT THE YMCA
Abbot/Haisley/Wines

400 West Washington St.
Ann Arbor, MI 48103
(734) 996-9622

Karate not only teaches self defense but its also good for developing balance, fitness, coordination, self-confidence and discipline. Shotokan karate primarily teaches through the practice of basic techniques and forms. The minimum age for students in this class is eight years old.

KELSEY MUSEUM OF ARCHAEOLOGY

Abbot/Haisley/Wines

434 South State St.
Ann Arbor, MI 48104

(734) 764-9304 | www.umich.edu

Exploration can be a fun and exciting activity with your son or daughter. Imagine the ability to explore ancient Egypt or the Mediterranean. The Kelsey Museum has over 100,000 objects from these civilizations on hand.

NEUTRAL ZONE

Abbot/Haisley/Wines

310 East Washington St.
Ann Arbor, MI 48104

(734) 214-9995 | www.neutral-zone.org

The Neutral Zone is a great place for children and a terrific resource for dads. The Zone's after-school education program provides a safe place for children to study complete with tutors and individual mentors to help guide children through the college process. Additional programs available at the Neutral Zone include literary art, visual art, music, and leadership.

ROBINSONGS FOR KIDS

Abbot/Haisley/Wines

1785 West Stadium Blvd.
Ann Arbor, MI 48103

(734) 929-2133 | www.robinsongsforkids.com

Robinsongs For Kids is as unique as the name suggests. This business was internationally recognized for its early childhood programs for babies, toddlers, preschoolers and kindergartners. The program promotes adults and children to share music in a non-performance setting. Be the dad who shares a special lifelong moment with your baby.

826 MICHIGAN

Abbot/Haisley/Wines

115 East Liberty St.
Ann Arbor, MI 48104

(734) 761-3463 | www.826michigan.org

This great Ann Arbor resource is the local arm of the 826 writing workshop organization that was started in San Francisco by acclaimed author Dave Eggers. They are an organization built on helping students ages 6 to 18 with their writing skills. They also help teachers to inspire their students to write. And their Robot Supply & Repair store gives creative writers an outlet, and curious kids lots of cool things to gawk at (and buy).

COBBLESTONE FARM MUSEUM

Allen, Bryant & Pattengill–East

2781 Packard Rd.
Ann Arbor, MI 48108
(734) 794-6230 | www.cobblestonefarms.org

Be the dad with the ability to travel back in time. Or, at least it may seem so. The mission of the Cobblestone Farm Association is to provide an example of a Washtenaw County farmstead circa 1845-1860.

UNIVERSITY MUSICAL SOCIETY

Allen, Bryant & Pattengill–East

881 North University Ave.
Ann Arbor, MI 48104
(734) 764-6833 | www.ums.org

Ann Arbor is filled with world-class cultural and educational opportunities. Be the dad who broadens his child's horizon by introducing the Grammy Award-winning world of the Ann Arbor Symphony Orchestra-Choral Union.

WIARD'S ORCHARDS AND COUNTY FAIR

Allen, Bryant & Pattengill–East

5565 Merritt Rd.
Ypsilanti, MI 48197
(734) 482-7744 | www.wiards.com

Wiard's 200-acre facility includes an orchard, a cider mill, country store and a bakery. The county fair is held on the grounds and runs from Wednesday through Sunday beginning in late September. The county fair can be an exciting place for children young and old. This fair is complete with a corn maze, straw mountains and hay rides. On the weekend, activities include clowns, face painting, pony rides, sand art and, candle dipping. Be the dad remembered for going to the county fair.

TUBA CHRISTMAS

Burns Park – East & Carpenter

University of Michigan
800 North University St.
Ann Arbor, MI 48108
(734) 395-9544

Is your child a music lover? Well, this is a must-do. This free annual event brings together over 40 tubas and euphonium players in a fun and festive musical showcase. Dress warmly and come enjoy a Tuba Christmas in Ann Arbor.

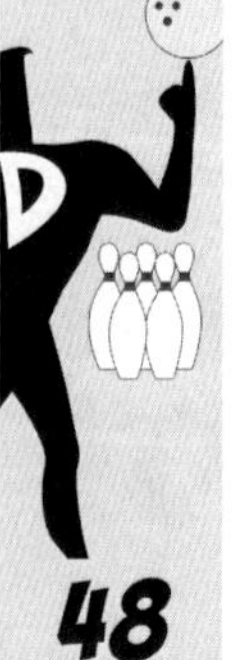

SACRED SONG

Mitchel & Pittsfield

Temple Beth Emeth
2309 Packard Rd.
Ann Arbor, MI 48104
(734) 973-6779 | www.waymaking.com

There is nothing like live music to set the right mood. Sacred Song is a multi-ethnic choral group who has been performing a December concert since 1995. Their rhythmic sounds affirm the values of social justice and spiritual inclusiveness. Everyone is welcome to celebrate, sing along, and enjoy music and rhythms from around the world. The requested donation is $20 per ticket at the door. The pre-sale ticket price is $15 and is available at the Women's Center of Southeastern Michigan. Admission is free for children under 12.

ANN ARBOR DISTRICT LIBRARY

Bryant/Pattengill – West/
Dickens/Lakewood/Lawton

343 South Fifth Ave.
Ann Arbor, MI 48104
(734) 327-4200 | www.aadl.org

All heroes know that the library is a cool place to be. Be the dad who knows it, too. The Ann Arbor District Library is not only a great source of information, but a great place for children to learn and be enriched by the programs and all of the available knowledge at your fingertips. Growing up, my mother created a neighborhood story time. It was the highlight of our week and every child in the neighborhood sat in while she read animated literary works. This same kind of story time is available at the library. It's a must-do because it will truly enrich their lives.

THE BEST DAD/CHILD
STORES

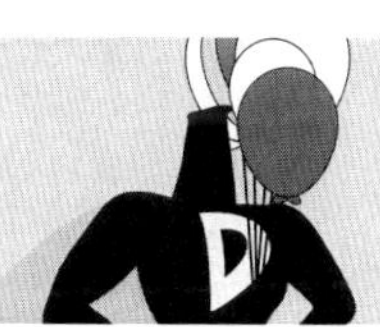

BIVOUAC
Angell

336 South State St.
Ann Arbor, MI 48104

(734) 761-6207 | www.bivouacannarbor.com

This is the store where all of the happening dads go to outfit everyone from infants to young adults with authentic outdoor gear. That's right—you can take your baby camping in style.

BORDERS
Angell

612 East Liberty St.
Ann Arbor, MI 48104

(734) 668-7652 | www.borders.com

This is the place where heroes or dad can find the kid's teaching zone, kid's music, kids' & family DVDs, used kid's books, kid's crafts, puzzles, games, toys & activity kits. Open: Monday-Saturday 10-a.m.10p.m.; Sunday 10a.m.-9p.m.

COLDSTONE CREAMERY
Angell

3597 Washtenaw Ave.
Ann Arbor, MI 48104

(734) 975-9910 | www.coldstonecreamery.com

This is where all dads go to satisfy their son's or daughter's sweet tooth. Or perhaps, get a delicious reward for that perfect report card. It's also a great place to pick up the best ice cream birthday cake in town.

DOWNTOWN ANN ARBOR
Angell

605 South Main St.
Ann Arbor, MI 48104

(734) 668-7112 | www.mainSt.annarbor.org

The Main St. Area Association is a great resource for getting up-to-date information on happenings in downtown Ann Arbor. Be the dad with the inside track to what's happening.

ELEPHANT EARS
Angell

Kerrytown Market & Shops
415 North Fifth Ave.
Ann Arbor, MI 48104

(734) 622-9580 | www.elephantearsonline.com

Knowing where to buy unique clothes and gifts is one of the marks of a superhero dad. Elephant Ears is where you get that done. They sell children's apparel for ages newborn to 12 years old. Each item reflects a commitment to originality and fun while the fabrics are hand-dyed, durable, pre-shrunk, 100% cotton wash and wear. Open weekdays 10a.m.-7p.m.; Saturday 9a.m.-6p.m.; Sunday 11a.m.-6p.m.

FALLING WATER BOOKS & COLLECTIBLES

Angell

213 South Main St.
Ann Arbor, MI 48104
(734) 747-9810 | www.fallingwatermi.com

Be the dad who knows where to find unique, one-of-a-kind gifts that honor the uniqueness and individuality in all of us. At Falling Water Books, a large percentage of their stock comes from small companies and independent artists.

HANDS-ON STORE

Angell

220 East Ann St.
Ann Arbor, MI 48104
(734) 995-5439 | www.aahom.org

Be the dad who inspires his children to discover the wonders of science, math and technology. Like the name says, this is the place to get your hands on tons of things to do.

LEXI'S TOY BOX

Angell

328 South Ashley St.
Ann Arbor, MI 48104-1351
(734) 332-1101 | www.lexistoybox.com

Looking for a special one-of-a-kind gift? Be the dad who knows where to get it. Lexi's is an independently owned specialty toy store. Everything in the store has been carefully selected to inspire creativity, promote healthy play and spark the imagination. Open: Tues-Fri 11a.m.-6p.m.; Sat.10a.m.-6 p.m.

MICHIGAN THEATER

Angell

603 East Liberty St.
Ann Arbor, MI 48104
(734) 668-8463 | www.michtheater.org

Be the dad who knows where the past and the future collide. The Michigan Theater was constructed in the silent film era and offers tours of its historic grounds. The theater also has a state-of-the-art sound system, which is perfect for listening to modern films. The theater is also known for live music.

MIDDLE EARTH

Angell

1209 South University Ave. #2
Ann Arbor, MI 48104
(734) 769-1488 | www.middleearthgifts.com

Middle Earth has been a part of Ann Arbor traditions for over 40 years, selling gags, cards, gifts, toys, games and more with creativity and a cute sense of humor.

MORGAN & YORK
Angell

1928 Packard Rd.
Ann Arbor, MI 48104
(734) 662-0798 | www.bigtenmarket.com

Heroes always know where to get the latest in party supplies or the perfect theme for their son's or daughter's birthday. Be the dad who knows, too. Morgan & York is a store that offers the latest in theme supplies and a whole lot more.

WASHINGTON ST. GALLERY
Angell

306 South Main St.
Ann Arbor, MI 48104
(734) 761-2287 | www.wsg-art.com

Be the dad who sparks his child's imagination by adding culture to the mix. The Washington St. Gallery has an 11-year history of bringing the finest in contemporary paintings, sculptures, and ceramics to its walls.

TOYS "R" US
Bach

3725 Washtenaw Ave.
Ann Arbor, MI 48104
(734) 973-2850 | www.toysrus.com

Being the hero who brings home the latest and coolest toys is a no-brainer. Toys "R" Us is the leading kids' store for toys, video games, dolls, action figures, learning toys, building toys, baby & toddler toys, and much more.

WHOLE FOODS
Bach

3135 Washtenaw Ave.
Ann Arbor, MI 48104
(734) 975-4500 | www.wholeFoodsMarket.com

This is the place where WonderDad can make sure his family gets the highest-quality natural and organic products.

FOUR DIRECTIONS
Burns Park Central

329 South Main St.
Ann Arbor, MI 48104
(734) 996-9250 | www.fourdirectionsa2.com

Head to Four Directions when you are looking for where things from all over the world can be found in one location. Be the dad who always delivers the perfect gift for all occasions.

GREAT LAKES TEAM APPAREL

Eberwhite

309 South State St.
Ann Arbor, MI 48104

(734) 222-4047 | www.greatlakesteamapparel.com

If the phrase "Go Blue" or the winningest football program in NCAA Division I mean anything to you, then this would be the place to shop. The Team Apparel store has a full line of licensed Michigan gear. Be the dad who outfits his children in authentic Michigan apparel.

MODA BLUE

Eberwhite

5 Nickels Arcade
Ann Arbor, MI 48104

(734) 913-0130 | www.modablue.com

A dad knows the importance of finding that perfect dress or outfit for the perfect occasion. Be the dad who also knows where and how to get it done. Check out Moda Blue.

PEN IN HAND

Eberwhite

1014 Baldwin Ave.
Ann Arbor, MI 48104

(734) 662-7276 | www.peninhand.biz

Pen In Hand is an excellent place to go for all of your stationery needs. They do fabulous work with calligraphy and photographs. Be the dad who knows where to get the perfect invitations for any occasion.

TREE TOWN TOYS

Northside & Thurston

2611 Plymouth Rd.
Ann Arbor, MI 48105

(734) 929-6545 | www.treetowntoys.com

I can remember waking up one Christmas morning to find a red cedar fort and a free-standing treehouse with a sliding pole down the middle. I was so excited. I felt like I was stepping out on to the moon. I have no idea how my father and mother pulled it off. Tree Town toys offers fabulous toys that bring back all of those great memories. My brothers and I and every kid in the neighborhood had years of fun with those toys. Be the dad who makes his child's dreams come true.

ANNA BANANA

Abbot/Haisley/Wines

1103 South University (2nd Floor)
Ann Arbor, MI 48103

(734) 222-0755

Be the dad who encourages the individuality in all of us. No matter what your style, chances are you can find it at Ann Banana's and be thanked for your thoughtfulness. The store sports the best in new and used apparel.

CHILD'S ORCHARD

Abbot/Haisley/Wines

887 West Eisenhower Pkwy.
Ann Arbor, MI 48103

(734) 995-8889 | www.childrensorchard.com

The Orchard is where that budding hero can go to save money. This is the place where you go to buy or sell new and used children's name-brand clothing, toys, and accessories.

KING'S KEYBOARD HOUSE

Abbot/Haisley/Wines

2333 East Stadium Blvd.
Ann Arbor, MI 48104

(734) 663-3381 | www.kingskeyboard.com

One Christmas my little brother woke up to find a baby grand piano as his gift. He grew up to be a concert pianist. The piano and a lot of hard work made two dreams come true. King's Keyboard House has been an Ann Arbor fixture since 1961. They offer both new and used pianos as well as musical lessons.

NICOLA'S BOOKS

Abbot/Haisley/Wines

2603 Jackson Ave.
Ann Arbor, MI 48103

(734) 662-0600 | www.nicolasbooks.com

Books are windows to our past, present and future. Be the dad who knows the importance of a solid education and the role books play in a good education. Nicola's is a privately owned bookstore with a large selection of books to choose from. Additionally, Nicola's brings children's books to life with a live presentation and photo session of the characters in the book.

ONCE UPON A CHILD

Abbot/Haisley/Wines

3426 Washtenaw Ave.
Ann Arbor, MI 48104

(734) 971-6822 | www.ouac.com

The name practically speaks for itself. It's a unique and affordable way to reuse children's things that have child-tested experience and a recyclable life left.

BORDERS

Allen, Bryan & Pattengill – East

100 Phoenix Dr.
Ann Arbor, MI 48108

(734) 477-1100 | www.borders.com

Being a dad is a tough job. But not to worry, at Borders you can find the teaching zone, kid's music, kid's & family DVDs, used kid's books, kid's crafts, puzzles, games and toys & activity kits. Open: Monday-Saturday 10a.m.-10p.m.; Sunday 10a.m.-9p.m.

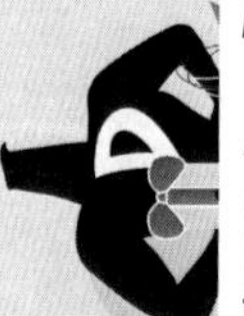

WIZZYWIG COLLECTIBLES

Allen, Bryan & Pattengill – East

4720 South State Rd.
Ann Arbor, MI 48108
(734) 213-1112 | www.wizzywig.com

This is where dads go to get the latest in Japanese anime CDs, DVDs, and video games. Wizzywig's also has an array of other products as well.

BUILD A BEAR WORKSHOP

Burns Park – East & Carpenter

404 Briarwood Cir.
Ann Arbor, MI 48108
(734) 761-2285 | www.buildabear.com

That stuffed animal your kid will sleep with until he or she goes off to college? It'll mean even more to them if you make it together. This store is a one-of-a-kind experience where you can choose from hundreds of designs and accessories.

DISCOVERY CHANNEL STORE

Mitchell & Pittsfield

100 Briarwood Cir.
Ann Arbor, MI 48108
(734) 769-8403 | www.store.discovery.com

The Discovery Channel Store is a wonderful and fascinating place to be. They have a plethora of things to help stimulate their imagination and put that never-ending grin on your children's faces. This is truly a one-of-a-kind, don't-miss-the-boat opportunity. Be the dad who does more than simply checks it out.

THE SCRAP BOX

Mitchell & Pittsfield

581 State Cir.
Ann Arbor, MI 48108
(734) 994-0012 | www.scrapbox.org

The Scrap Box is a secondhand creative reuse store. Instead of allowing used items from businesses and manufacturers to go to landfill The Scrap Box sends them back into circulation. Be the dad who knows a great deal when he sees one. The reusable items are great for art projects, science experiments, and handmade crafts.

FOOT PRINTS

Mitchell & Pittsfield

1200 South University Ave.
Ann Arbor, MI 48104
(734) 994-9401 | www.shopfootprints.com

Comfortable shoes are a necessity. Any dad who knows where to purchase the most comfortable shoes is well on his way to being a hero. Foots specializes in a wide range of name-brand shoes and designer sandals.

PARTY CITY

2857 Oak Valley Dr.
Ann Arbor, MI 48103
(734) 663-4663 | www.partycity.com

Bryant/Pattengill – West/
Dickens/Lakewood/Lawton

No kids' party is complete without balloons. Party City is the place to get balloons and a whole lot more. Be the dad who throws the coolest parties in town.

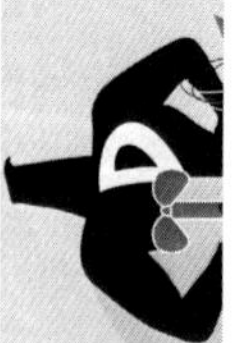

THE BEST DAD/CHILD
OUTDOOR PARKS & RECREATION

ANN ARBOR FARMERS' MARKET

Angell

Farmers' Market Pavilion
315 Detroit St.
Ann Arbor, MI 48104
(734) 794-6244

Show your child first hand what farm-grown produce is like. The market is nestled in historic Kerrytown and features locally grown food, plants, handcrafts, and prepared food items.

BURNS PARK

Bach

1300 Baldwin Ave.
Ann Arbor, MI 48104

This park is a 15-acre neighborhood park with quite a few amenities. There is a small shelter with restrooms, a drinking fountain, five tennis courts, a basketball court, a sledding hill, and an ice and hockey rink in the winter.

ESCH PARK

Bach

2741 Esch Ave.
Ann Arbor, MI 48104

This five-acre park sports two half basketball courts, a paved game court, tennis courts, play equipment, a softball field, benches and a large open field. The park is located off Fenwick St. between Packard Rd. and Eisenhower Pkwy.

WINCHELL PARK

Burns Park Central

2298 Winchell Dr.
Ann Arbor, MI 48104

Winchell Park is 4.5-acres and has a number of amenities. Besides the open field, there's a softball diamond, soccer goals, children's play equipment and picnic tables.

FRISINGER PARK

Eberwhite

1150 East Stadium Blvd.
Ann Arbor, MI 48104

This small neighborhood park is 3.6 acres. On hand is a play area, benches, picnic tables, barbeque grills, and a softball field. Be the dad who knows how much fun running free in the park can be.

BROMLEY PARK

King & Logan

2775 Briarcliff St.
Ann Arbor, MI 48105

This 2.5-acre park has a magnificent rose garden and brand-new play equipment. The park also has picnic tables and benches. This would be a terrific place for a family picnic.

CEDAR BEND NATURE AREA — King & Logan

1472 Cedar Bend Dr.
Ann Arbor, MI 48105

This is Ann Arbor's oldest park. The 19-acre park is home to a large variety of plant life to include skunk cabbage, jack-in-the pulpit and alternate leaf dogwood. Facilities are available in nearby Island Park, where there are picnic spots along the river.

FULLER RECREATION AREA — King & Logan

1519 Fuller Rd.
Ann Arbor, MI 48105

This 60-acre park is an exciting place to be. The soccer fields are where the Ann Arbor Soccer Association plays. There are also a number of other great amenities like a 50-meter outdoor pool, a water slide, restroom, and locker room facilities and a concession stand, which operates in the summer. Additionally, the play area is one of the largest in the city with picnic tables located nearby.

GALLUP PARK — King & Logan

3000 Fuller Rd.
Ann Arbor, MI 48105
(734) 994-2780

This is Ann Arbor's park of choice. The 69-acre park is located along the Huron River and Geddes Pond. There are beautiful scenic walkways throughout the park. The park has two playgrounds, a canoe livery, picnic areas, barbeque grills, two picnic shelters, open fields, and three miles of paved asphalt where you often see people biking, rollerblading, walking, and running.

ARGO CANOE LIVERY — Northside & Thurston

1055 Longshore Dr.
Ann Arbor, MI 48105
(734) 668-7411 |

The Livery is home to over 100 canoes, rowboats and kayaks. This is a great place to sit and become one with nature. They also offer summer camps for 6th, 7th and 8th graders who want to become paddling experts!

ALLMENDINGER PARK — Abbot/Haisley/Wines

Pauline Blvd.
Ann Arbor, MI 48103

Allmendinger is an eight-acre neighborhood park with a number of amenities. The park has a softball field, restrooms, water fountain, children's play area, picnic tables, a tennis court, a grass volleyball court, and a basketball court.

BIRD'S HILL NATURE AREA

Abbot/Haisley/Wines

Bird Rd. off Huron River & M-14
Ann Arbor, MI 48103

This is Ann Arbor's largest park and a hiker's or nature lover's paradise. It's also a great place to photograph wildlife in its natural surroundings.

CAMP AL-GON-QUIAN

Abbot/Haisley/Wines

400 West Washington St.
Ann Arbor, MI 48103
(734) 996-9622

Camp Al-Gon-Quian is the YMCA's overnight camp for children starting age 6 through 16. The camp is located on Burt Lake in Northern Michigan and has 85 years of history and tradition.

FLAG FOOTBALL AT THE YMCA

Abbot/Haisley/Wines

400 West Washington St.
Ann Arbor, MI 48103
(734) 996-9622

Flag football is an excellent way to learn the finer points of gridiron glory without the physical contact. This one-hour-long sessions are geared toward ages 6 and up and starts by teaching the basics of throwing and catching and builds on the basic skills needed to compete in the Y's flag football league.

FOOTBALL AT THE YMCA

Abbot/Haisley/Wines

400 West Washington St.
Ann Arbor, MI 48103
(734) 996-9622

One of my favorite activities growing up was playing football. Help teach your child the finer points of America's game. I know there are some that would argue that it's baseball or perhaps basketball, but it's football.

HIGH POINT SCHOOL ABLE TO PLAY PLAYGROUND

Abbot/Haisley/Wines

1735 South Wagner Rd.
Ann Arbor, MI 48103
www.michigan.org

Be the hero who takes your child to a playground they never want to leave. A playground with twisty slides, swings, sand boxes and shade trees is a child's dreamland.

NETBALL AT THE YMCA
Abbot/Haisley/Wines

400 West Washington St.
Ann Arbor, MI 48103
(734) 996-9622

Be the dad who's on the cutting edge of a new sports trend. Netball is a new and exciting team sport for your daughter to learn and play. They say it's one of the fastest growing sports in Australia and New Zealand. The game involves passing a ball between teammates who try and score against their opponents. This game helps teach great teamwork and sportsmanship. The sport is geared toward ages 7 and up.

SOCCER AT THE YMCA
Abbot/Haisley/Wines

400 West Washington St.
Ann Arbor, MI 48103
(734) 996-9622

Soccer has always been big in Europe and for that matter most of the rest of the world. However, it does have quite a bit of popularity in many communities. The learn-to-play soccer program helps children starting at age 5 learn the skills of passing, dribbling and shooting in a safe, fun and secure atmosphere.

STREET HOCKEY
Abbot/Haisley/Wines

400 West Washington St.
Ann Arbor, MI 48103
(734) 996-9622

Being close to "Hockey Town" has its advantages. The Detroit Redwings sponsor a street hockey program. Be the dad who helps to introduce his budding hockey player to a life-long sport. The program helps develop superior hand-to-eye coordination and is geared toward ages 4 and up.

YMCA
Abbot/Haisley/Wines

400 West Washington St.
Ann Arbor, MI 48103
(734) 996-9622 | www.annarborymca.org

The fantastic part about sports is that it provides your child with several valuable lessons. The YMCA is one of the best places to find teams and leagues to get your youngsters started learning and competing just about any sport you can imagine. They also have summer day and overnight camps, after-school programs, and all sorts of parent/child activities. Plus, family memberships are a bargain, and you can work out, swim, or take a class of your own while the kids are at practice.

BANDEMER PARK

Allen, Bryant & Pattengill – East

1352 Lakeshore Dr.
Ann Arbor, MI 48104-1057

(734) 994-2780 | www.a2gov.org

This 37-acre park has a number of great amenities. The park offers restrooms, benches, and an accessible canoe dock, fishing deck, shelters, picnic areas, and barbeque grills. Be the dad who delivers on the total package.

BUHR PARK

Allen, Bryant & Pattengill – East

2751 Packard Rd.
Ann Arbor, MI 48108

This park features 39 acres of rolling hills, picnic areas, barbeque grills, a child's play area, a softball field, soccer fields, and an outdoor tennis court. The signature feature at the park is a 25-yard, six-lane pool with a deep well. There is also a zero-depth-entry pool with interactive play toys for children.

DELHI METROPOLITAN PARK

Burns Park – East & Carpenter

3902 East Delhi Rd.
Ann Arbor, MI 48108

(734) 426-8211 | www.metropark.com

Ann Arbor's Delhi Park is an exciting place to visit with your son or daughter. The park has every activity available from A to Z. This is an absolute must-be place to visit at least once. Smarts dads will make it more than once.

VETERAN'S MEMORIAL INDOOR ICE ARENA & POOL

Mitchell & Pittsfield

2105 Jackson Pl.
Ann Arbor, MI 48103

(734) 761-7240 | www.a2gov.org

If you're a kid and you live in Ann Arbor, this is the place to cool off during the summer. The facility has a large water slide, diving board, and a pool for little ones. In addition, they have all sorts of sprinklers to help you stay cool.

MACK INDOOR POOL

715 Brooks St.
Ann Arbor, MI 48103
(734) 994-2898 | www.a2gov.org

This is a great place for children to learn how to swim. The facility offers public swimming and swimming programs in its six-lane, 25-yard indoor main pool with an attached 30-foot-by-42-foot children's pool. Learning to swim is an awesome adventure. Be the dad who leads the way to adventure and excitement.

THE BEST DAD/CHILD
SPORTING EVENTS

ANN ARBOR AMATEUR HOCKEY ASSOCIATION

Angell

301 East Liberty St.
Ann Arbor, MI 48104-2262
(734) 222-0071 | www.annarbor.com

For six years, I worked as a sports editor and one of the sports I reported on was amateur hockey. The joy and excitement parents and the children got out of re-living their exploits in print left me in amazement. This truly is a dad/son and, yes, daughter, moment. The AAAHA offers noncompetitive beginners programs for ages 4-7 and instructional programs for ages 8-17 with spring, fall, and winter seasons.

COLONIAL LANES

Burns Park Central

1950 South Industrial
Ann Arbor, MI 48104
(734) 665-4474 | www.bowldetroit.com

Bowling can be a unique sport, especially if Dad participates. The bowling center provides hours of family recreation and fun. One of the more popular activities is birthday parties. Open bowling is Monday-Wednesday 9a.m.-midnight; Thursday-Saturday 9a.m.-2a.m.; Sunday 11a.m.-midnight.

ANN ARBOR FIELD HOCKEY CLUB (AAFHC)

Eberwhite

1000 South State St.
Ann Arbor, MI 48104
(734) 764-2144 | www.michiganfieldhockeycamp.com

This underappreciated game requires the participants to be in great physical condition. The AAFHC offers training session throughout the year for children ages 9-18 with overnight and commuter summer camps for high school players.

U-M NORTH CAMPUS RECREATION CENTER

King & Logan

2375 Hubbard Dr.
Ann Arbor, MI 48109
(248) 763-4560 | www.unmich.edu

The North Campus Recreation Center is the place to go to talk turkey. This is the site where the annual Turkey Trot takes place. In addition, the center has a swimming pool, personal exercise equipment, and a rock climbing wall. Be the dad who knows how to cover all bases.

SPORTING EVENTS

I9 SPORTS
WASHTENAW COUNTY

Northside & Thurston

3976 Warren Ct.
Ann Arbor, MI 48105
(734) 302-7529 | www.i9sports.com

I9 Sports is an exciting franchise which involves children, sports, and dads. The franchises have active youth flag football, cheerleading, basketball, and soccer leagues. Be the dad who does more than sit on the side lines. Instructional classes are for children ages 5 through 12 years old with fall and winter classes available.

CHAMPION GYMNASTICS

Abbot/Haisley/Wines

240 Metty Dr., Suite C
Ann Arbor, MI 48103
(734) 222-1810 | www.championgymnasticsannarbor.com

Championship Gymnastics offers something for the gymnast is all of us. They have an 8-week recreational class for children 18 months and over, team programs and field trips. Their one-week summer camp is for children ages 4 and up with half- and full-day options.

ANN ARBOR
TRACK CLUB

Allen, Bryant & Pattengill – East

P.O. Box 7551
Ann Arbor, MI 48107
(734) 332-9129 | www.aatrackclub.org

Be the dad who knows there's a purpose to running everywhere. Ann Arbor also offers a youth track club. The track club offers a competitive and non-competitive league for children ages 6-18. The indoor season runs between November and March and the outdoor season is April to August with the cross-country season going from August to December.

ANN ARBOR AREA BASEBALL
ASSOCIATION

Allen, Bryant & Pattengill – East

(734) 678-4358 | www.aaaba.20m.com

Headed by President Dan Kielczewski, this league features games and tournaments for ages 9 through 16. The spring and summer season starts in late April and runs through mid-July. The fall seasons starts in late August and lasts until mid-October. These guys recently joined forces with the Washtenaw Amateur Baseball Association, a travel league for children ages 9-16, comprised of teams from Washtenaw and nearby counties.

SPRING T-BALL AT PITTSFIELD PARKS & REC

Allen, Bryant & Pattengill – East

(734) 822-2120

The Pittsfield Township Parks and Recreation offers a spring T-ball league for children ages 5-8. Registration starts in February.

WASHTENAW JUNIOR FOOTBALL PROGRAM

Allen, Bryant & Pattengill – East

(734) 218-0287 | www.washtenawjrfootball.org

Find competitive football and high-quality instruction with no tryouts or cuts in this great program for tiny tacklers. Teams compete in the Downriver Junior Football League from August through November. They also have a junior cheer squad to get your little girls involved as well.

CLUB WOLVERINE SWIM TEAM

Allen, Bryant & Pattengill – East

P.O. Box 130229
Ann Arbor, MI 48113
(734) 332-9440 | www.clubwolverine.org

The swimming club offers year-round programs to help children develop as swimmers. The programs are specifically designed for children ages 4-18. The Wolverine Club is a member and sanctioned by USA swimming.

GREAT LAKES WATER POLO CLUB

Allen, Bryant & Pattengill – East

Canham Natatorium
500 East Hoover St.
Ann Arbor, MI 48104
(734) 764-6545 | www.greatlakeswaterpolo.com

Be the dad who gets the early start. Water Polo is an exciting sport. The Canham Natatorium is home to a lot of history and success. The University of Michigan-based program offers year-round programs, something for the younger crowd, and clinics for high school students.

LIBERTY ATHLETIC CLUB

Allen, Bryant & Pattengill – East

3975 West Liberty Rd.
Ann Arbor, MI 48103
(734) 665-3738 | www.libertyathletic.net

The Liberty Club is the perfect place for children to improve their coordination. The classes incorporate tumbling, stretching, obstacle courses, ball games, and ballet and are specifically designed for children ages 3-5. Classes designed for children ages 4-12 include basic training in ballet and other fitness programs.

MERI LOU MURRAY RECREATION CENTER
Allen, Bryant & Pattengill – East

2960 Washtenaw Ave.
Ann Arbor, MI 48104
(734) 971-6355 | www.a2gov.org/park

The recreation center is wheelchair accessible, has a 25-yard pool, track, weight room, badminton, basketball, volleyball, and pickle ball courts in addition to cardio and strength training equipment for children age 16 and older.

MICHIGAN ACADEMY OF GYMNASTICS
Allen, Bryant & Pattengill – East

3900 Jackson Rd., Suite 4
Ann Arbor, MI 48103
(734) 761-7610 | www.michiganacademy.com

The Michigan Academy of Gymnast has programs for children age 2 and up, which include preschool movement, and developmental and competitive gymnastics. They also offer gymnastics summer camps.

PLANET ROCK
Allen, Bryant & Pattengill – East

82 Aprill Dr. #B
Ann Arbor, MI 48103
(734) 827-2680 | www.planet-rock.com

Have you ever thought it would be cool to take your son or daughter rock-climbing? Well, Planet Rock has climbing programs for children of all ages and abilities. The ABCs of rock climbing are agility, balance and coordination. The Climbing Center has classes starting for children ages 3-6 and weekly climbing clubs for children ages 7-15. There are also competitive climbing teams for children ages 9-19.

U-MOVE FITNESS
Allen, Bryant & Pattengill – East

401 Washtenaw Ave.
Ann Arbor, MI 48109
(734) 764-1342 | www.kines.umich.edu/umove/kidsport

U-Move fitness is a seven-week summer physical education program for children ages 4-15. The morning activities are swimming, team sports, games, and safety instruction. The afternoons feature one-week sessions in golf, tennis, baseball, basketball, soccer, track and field, and other sports.

UNIVERSITY OF MICHIGAN STADIUM

Allen, Bryant & Pattengill – East

701 Tappan Ave.
Ann Arbor, MI 48108
(734) 764-1817 | www.umich.edu

The University of Michigan has a great array of summer camps and clinics available for youths. They have both commuter and overnight camps for youth in all-sport to help improve speed and agility, baseball, basketball, cross country, diving, field hockey, football, golf, gymnastics, ice hockey, rowing, soccer, softball, swimming, tennis, track and field, volleyball, water polo, wrestling, lacrosse, and strength and conditioning skills. For additional information, visit them at www.mgoblue.com.

WOLVERINE FOOTBALL AT THE BIG HOUSE

Allen, Bryant & Pattengill – East

701 Tappan Ave.
Ann Arbor, MI 48108
(734) 764-1817 | www.mgoblue.com

Watching a Michigan Wolverine football game with your kids, and 105,000 of your neighbors, all screaming at the top of your lungs in the crisp fall air is one of the all-time greatest moments for a WonderDad, especially if junior turns to you mid-way through the third quarter and says, "Dad, I want to play quarterback for Michigan when I grow up!" It can only happen if you plan ahead, despite the enormous stadium, these are the hottest tickets in town.

WOLVERINE ALL STAR CHEER

Allen, Bryant & Pattengill – East

3460 East Ellsworth Rd.
Ann Arbor, MI 48108
(734) 395-8496 | www.wolverineallstar.com

The Wolverine All Star Cheer has a little something for everyone. They offer tumbling for cheerleaders classes, junior and senior teams, a competitive travel program and a special-needs program for all ages and abilities

WOLVERINE WRESTLING CLUB

Allen, Bryant & Pattengill – East

Crisler Arena
333 East Stadium St.
Ann Arbor, MI 48109
www.wolverinewrestlingclub.com

The Wolverine Wrestling Club meets at the University of fMichigan Crisler Arena. The Club offers professional instruction from U of M wrestlers, as well as summer camps for grade school through high school students. Club wrestlers also regularly compete in state, regional, and national tournaments.

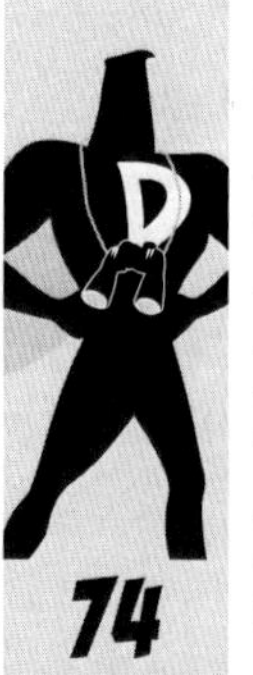

GYM AMERICA

Burns Park – East & Carpenter

4611 Platt Rd.
Ann Arbor, MI 48108
(734) 971-1667 | www.gymamericgymnastics.com

Gym America has an excellent program for children of all experience levels starting at 18 months and up. The summer camps and classes are completely supervised with an open gym for preschoolers. Another program, Gym America on Wheels, brings equipment and staff to schools and other locations to teach classes. They sponsor a noncompetitive and competitive gymnastics teams.

HURON VALLEY VOLLEYBALL CLUBS

Mitchell & Pittfield

2109 Stone School Cir.
Ann Arbor, MI 48108
(734) 975-0362 | www.huronvalleyvb.com

Be the dad who helps build your son or daughter's stamina, strength and hand-to-eye coordination through learning to play volleyball. The Huron Valley Volleyball Club offers programs for boys and girls ages 8-18 in all skill levels. They have year-round training, team competitions, and USAV/AAU/JVDA tournaments, clinics, and camps who play locally, regionally, and nationally.

WHIRLY BALL OF ANN ARBOR

Mitchell & Pittfield

750 Phoenix Dr.
Ann Arbor, MI 48108
(734) 975-6909 | www.whirlyballannarbor.com

Be the dad who knows how to party. If you like basketball, Jai-Alai and bumper cars, then you'll love whirly ball.

WIDEWORLD SPORTS CENTER

Bryant/Pattengill – West/
Dickens/Lakewood/Lawton

2140 Oak Valley Dr.
Ann Arbor, MI 48103
(734) 913-4625 | www.wideworld-sports.com

The Wideworld Sports Center is a state-of-the-art indoor soccer and lacrosse arena where children can compete and learn. The arena is home to over 1,100 soccer teams yearly. The Center's instructional programs are geared for children age 2 and up.

DETROIT TIGERS

Comerica Park
2100 Woodward Ave.
Detroit, MI 48201
(313) 962-4000 | www.detroit.tigers.mlb.com

Baseball is considers America's game and the Tigers have won the World Series four times. There's nothing like watching a live ballgame in the stands with Dad.

DETROIT PISTONS

The Palace of Auburn Hills
Five Championship Dr.
Auburn Hills, MI 48326
(248) 377-0100 | www.nba.com/pistons

The Detroit Pistons are three-time NBA Champions having won the title in 1989, 1990, and 2004. They always have a competitive team. Take your son or daughter to a professional basketball game.

DETROIT LIONS

2000 Brush St., Suite 200
Detroit, MI 48226
(313) 262-2000 | www.detroitlions.com

The Detroit Lions have won the NFL Championship four times. They captured the title in 1935, 1952, 1953, and 1957. They have struggled somewhat in recent years, but they're always trying. Be the dad who supports the home team.

DETROIT REDWINGS

Joe Louis Arena
600 Civic Center Dr.
Detroit, MI 48226
(313) 396-7444 | www.redwings.nhl.com

A trip to see a professional sports team play in person is something to remember. Everything from getting popcorn, soda and candy to where you sat with your dad is noteworthy. The Redwings are the standard-bearers for the NHL. They have brought home the Stanley Cup 11 times. Be the dad who sees his games live—at least once.

TOLEDO MUD HENS

Fifth Third Field
406 Washington St.
Toledo, OH 43604
(419) 725-4367 | www.minorleaguebaseball.com

Believe it or not, a minor league baseball game is a great father-daughter activity. Minor league baseball is its own brand of exciting. The minor league clubs are feeder programs for the big leagues. If you log on to www.minorleaguebaseball.com you will find every minor league team. Click on the Toledo Mud Hens name for a direct link. The Mud Hens are 53 miles from Ann Arbor.

THE BEST DAD/CHILD
UNIQUE ADVENTURES

KERRYTOWN CONCERT HOUSE Angell

415 North Fourth Ave.
Ann Arbor, MI 48104
(734) 769-2999 | www.kerrytownconcerthouse.com
The Kerrytown Concert House is a historic Victorian home with an intimate feel. The venue features everything from classical to experimental music. Be the dad who adds a little class and grace to his child's life.

JUMP CITY Bach

2825 Boardwalk
Ann Arbor, MI 48104
(734) 995-5055 | www.jump-city.com
Jump City is the place for the kid in all of us. Be the dad who knows how to entertain children from age 2 and up. Socks are required on your feet and lots of energy.

BARNES & NOBLE BOOKSELLERS Burns Park Central

Huron Village-3235 Washtenaw Ave.
Ann Arbor, MI 48104
(734) 973-0846 | www.barnesandnoble.com
Be big part of being a kid is the ability to dream. Heroes encourage children to dream. One of the unique projects available at Barnes & Noble allows children to create their own stories and turn them into their own books. Be that dad!

URBAN FAIRY DOORS Eberwhite

Downtown Ann Arbor
(734) 995-7281 | www.urban-fairies.com
Do you believe in fairies? Well, there's proof that fairies do exist in Ann Arbor; at least that's what some people say. One of the more unique adventures to explore is the legend of Urban Fairy Doors. What are fairy doors? Fairy doors are tiny doors built into the interior or exterior of a building. There are restaurants, stores, and even a school around Ann Arbor with fairy doors just waiting to be discovered. Some of those places are listed below...Be the dad who wants to share this mystery firsthand with their son or daughter.

ANN ARBOR FRAMING COMPANY Eberwhite

838 South Main St.
Ann Arbor, MI 48104
(734) 741-8656
Rumor has it that someone is building the fairy doors. But, that's only an ugly rumor. You can view the little doors at the Framing Company.

JEFFERSON MARKET
Eberwhite

609 West Jefferson St.
Ann Arbor, MI 48103
(734) 665-6666 | www.jeffersonmarketandcakery.com

This is a market where you can buy produce and baked goods. In all shapes and sizes. They also have some tiny doors.

LAKEWOOD ELEMENTARY
Eberwhite

344 Gralake Ave.
Ann Arbor, MI 48103
(734) 994-1953 | www.a2schools.org/lakewood.home

This is the location for higher learning and tiny doors. We aren't talking about doors for small children; these doors are a little bit smaller. But, don't visit the school; they're busy teaching the children.

SELO SHEVEL GALLERY
Eberwhite

301 South Main St.
Ann Arbor, MI 48104
(734) 761-6263 | www.seloshevelgallery.com

This is a fantastic art gallery with lots of neat stuff, including tiny doors. Please go to check out their artwork.

SWEETWATER'S CAFÉ
Eberwhite

123 West Washington St.
Ann Arbor, MI 48104
(734) 769-2331 | www.sweetwaterscafe.com

This is a great place to have lunch if you are in downtown Ann Arbor. However, be careful not to drop any crumbs on the floor.

THE ARK
Eberwhite

316 South Main St.
Ann Arbor, MI 48104
(734) 761-1818 | www.theark.org

The Ark is a gift shop in downtown Ann Arbor. They have lots of unique one-of-a-kind gifts and a few tiny doors somewhere in the building.

PEACEABLE KINGDOM
Eberwhite

210 South Main St.
Ann Arbor, MI 48104
(734) 668-7886 | www.theaapk.com

Peaceable Kingdom is a gift store. However, if you decide to visit, just be sure not to leave any tiny doors standing open.

GERALD R. FORD PRESIDENTIAL LIBRARY

King & Logan

1000 Beal Ave.
Ann Arbor, MI 48105
(734) 205-0555

The Gerald R. Ford Presidential Library is housed on the campus of President Ford's alma mater (B.A. 1935), the University of Michigan. The library houses all of President Ford's White House papers from 1974 to 1977. Be the dad who helps his son or daughter learn about our shared history and the political process up close.

GIANT CAMPUS SUMMER CAMPS

Northside & Thurston

(888) 904-2267 | www.giantcampus.com

We live in a computer-friendly world. Be the dad who helps his son or daughter get a jump or leg up in today's world. Giant Campus offers single and multi-week computer camps in game design, web design, animation, and video production. Classes are geared toward students ages 6-17.

HURON SCUBA ADVENTURES

Abbot/Haisley/Wines

4816 Jackson Rd., Suite D
Ann Arbor, MI 48103
(734) 994-3483 | www.huronscuba.com

My first experience with SCUBA diving came in a tropical paradise. I was fortunate enough to win an all-inclusive, 10-day, paid trip to Nassau. Be the dad who can share a truly unique and fantastic world with his son or daughter without the long distance travel. SCUBA diving is a world unto itself. An added plus at Huron SCUBA is the kids' SCUBA birthday party and the classes for beginners.

ZAP ZONE

Allen, Bryant & Pattengill – Easy

2809 Boardwalk St.
Ann Arbor, MI 48104
(734) 933-6670 | www.zap-zone.com

Help build a healthy competitive spirit by playing laser tag or riding in go-carts at the Zap Zone. The Zap Zone is the ultimate party environment.

ROLLING HILLS FAMILY WATER PARK

Burns Park – East & Carpenter

7660 Stony Creek Rd.
Ypsilanti, MI 48197
(734) 484-9676 | www.parks.ewashtenaw.org

This family water park is in Ann Arbor's backyard. It's a 6.5-acre facility with a wave and activities pool, water slides, lazy river, children's spray play area and concession stands. Admission is free to anyone under 36 inches tall.

AJS FAMILY FUN CENTER

4400 Ball Park Dr., Northeast
Grand Rapids, MI 48838
(231) 843-4838 | www.ajsfamilyfun.com

This family fun center has tons of kid-friendly indoor fun things to do. Be the hero who creates those lasting dad/son/daughter memories. The center is only 177 kilometers from Ann Arbor.

FISHING IN ALCONA PARK

2550 AuSable River Rd.
Glennie, MI 48737
(989) 735-3881 | www.alconapark.com

Be the dad who knows where to go fishing. Alcona Park has over 1,100 acres and three miles of shoreline perfectly suited for catching that once-in-a-lifetime trophy or a fish tale for the ages. The park is 120 miles from Ann Arbor.

ALFRED P. SLOAN MUSEUM

1221 East Kearsley St.
Flint, MI 48503
(810) 237-3450 | www.sloanmuseum.com

If unique is what you seek, then this is your museum to frequent. At the Science Discovery Center, children can explore hands-on scientific principles of both chemistry and physics. This is a must-do for every aspiring hero. The museum is 40 miles from Ann Arbor.

ANDY T'S FAMILY FUN FARM

3131 South US-27
St. John, MI 48879
(989) 224-7674

Think you might enjoy going to a working farm for the weekend. Well, Andy's Farm is a family-oriented fresh fruit and vegetable market. They have hayrides, a petting farm and a 6-acre corn maze. Additionally, you can make and enjoy your own caramel apples. Andy's is just 70 miles from Ann Arbor.

AUTOMOTIVE HALL OF FAME

21400 Oakwood Blvd.

Detroit, MI 48124

(313) 240-4000 | www.automotivehalloffame.org

Detroit was home to the big three in automobiles during the heyday of car manufacturing. So it's fitting that the Hall of Fame is in Detroit. The museum is an excellent educational opportunity and creates to perfect bond between dad son/daughter and car.

AVALANCHE BAY INDOOR WATER PARK

1 Boyne Mountain Rd.

Boyne Falls, MI 49713

(231) 549-7979 | www.avalanchebay.com

Avalanche Bay is a quite a one-day trip by itself, but well worth the journey. The water park is Michigan's largest at 88,000 square feet of kid-tested and dad-approved water fun.

BESSER MUSEUM

491 Johnson St.

Alpena, MI 49707

(989) 356-2202 | www.bessermuseum.org

So the story goes...where can you find a Picasso, Indian artifacts, two Renoirs, lots of stuffed Michigan mammals, and the pump that fought the Chicago fires in one place—Alpena, of course. The Besser is located about 200 miles from Ann Arbor.

BIG BEAR ADVENTURES

4271 South Straits Hwy.

Indian River, MI 49749

(231) 238-8181 | www.bigbearadventures.com

Campfires songs, marshmallows, ghost stories, rafting, and getting back to nature are all in the preview of what it is to be Dad. Big Bear Adventures is the perfect outdoor family fun getaway.

CAMPING WITH THE KIDS

While camping WonderDad gets to teach his kids about self-reliance, determination, and the great outdoors. They'll probably learn all that just watching you put up the tent. Whether you are the dad who likes to hunt and fish or just sing songs and make s'mores by the campfire, campgrounds can become semi-sacred places in the minds of your children if you treat them right. Time spent camping has great positvie outcomes. There are 13 campgrounds within a 20-mile radius of Ann Arbor.

CEDAR POINT

1 Cedar Point Dr.
Sandusky, Ohio 44870
(419) 627-2350 | www.cedarpoint.com
Taking your kids to Cedar Point is hands down a day they will remember. The park has a total of 17 roller coaster rides, which is more than any other park in the world. The trip from Ann Arbor is about 110 miles or about a two-hour ride.

CROSSROADS VILLAGE & HUCKLEBERRY RAILROAD

5045 Stanley Rd.
Flint, MI 48506
(810) 736-7100 | www.geneseecountryparks.org
All aboard as the Huckleberry Railroad travels back in time. Experience the way folks traveled in the early 1900s on a scenic, 40-minute train ride. The Crossroads is only 55 miles from Ann Arbor.

CURIOUS KIDS MUSEUM

415 Lake Blvd.
St. Joseph, MI 49085
(269) 983-2543 | www.curiouskidsmuseum.org
Help satisfy the curiosity in your kids. The museum was designed to help stimulate the imagination with tons of hands-on activities. The museum is about 150 miles from Ann Arbor.

DEANNA'S PLAYHOUSE

11172 Adams St.
Holland, MI 49423
(616) 396-7566 | www.DeannasPlayhouse.com
This awesome playground is where imagination meets fantasy. The 15,000-square-foot multi-purpose center was designed to promote the power of play between parents and children. The playhouse is 130 miles from Ann Arbor.

DEER ACRES STORYBOOK AMUSEMENT PARK

2346 M-13
Pinconning, MI 48650
(989) 879-2849 | www.deeracres.com
At Deer Acres, Mother Goose rules! It's a child's fantasyland that's only 110 miles from Ann Arbor. Read a Mother goose story or two aloud on the drive over, and soon enough, your kids can be inside that very same story.

DETROIT HISTORICAL MUSEUM

5401 Woodward Ave.
Detroit, MI 48202
(313) 833-1805 | www.detroithistorical.org

The ability to reach out and touch living history waits for the inquisitive mind as this museum is home to over 600 historical artifacts; and more than 80,000 square feet of exhibition space. It was built in 1928 and remains as one of America's oldest museums. The museum is only 30 miles from Ann Arbor.

DETROIT SCIENCE CENTER

5020 John R
Detroit, MI 48202
(313) 577-8400 | www.sciencedetroit.org

Science is cool at this updated, hands-on, all-ages place to learn. The Science Center has a dome theatre, live science demonstrations, and a planetarium. Plus it is only 30 miles from Ann Arbor.

DETROIT ZOO

8450 West 10-Mile Rd.
Royal Oak, MI 48067
(248) 541-5717| www.detroitzoo.org

The Detroit Zoo is home to more than 270 species, and is a great place to build a passion for nature and science in your kids. Plus, they have wolverines, rhinos, and other super-cool animals. The zoo is only 35 miles from Ann Arbor.

DIAMOND JACK'S RIVER TOURS

114 Willow Dr.
Detroit, MI 48138
(313) 843-9316 | www.diamondjack.com

Take a cruise on the world's busiest international waterway. Be the dad who knows what cruising is all about. Diamond Jack's is 30 miles from Ann Arbor.

DOUBLE JJ RANCH & WATERPARK

5900 Water Rd.
Rothbury, MI 49452
1 (800) 368-2235 | www.doublejj.com

Superheroes go horseback riding with their son or daughter, and then turn right back around and take them on the tallest indoor slide in Michigan. Without question, the Double JJ is a place to be. The Ranch is 160 miles from Ann Arbor.

FULL BLAST

35 Hamblin Ave.
Battle Creek, MI 49017
(269) 966-3431 | www.fullblast.org
Battle Creek is more than just the headquarters for Kellogg's breakfast cereal. It's also a place where children can have indoor and outdoor seasonal water fun. The water theme park is only 75 miles from Ann Arbor.

GARLYN ZOOLOGICAL PARK

W9104 US-2
Naubinway, MI 49762
(906) 477-1085 | www.garlynzoo.com
Garlyn's is a little bit of a hike from Ann Arbor at more than 300 miles away, but well worth the trip. The park features animals and birds from all over the world, including a wide variety of America's wildlife.

GRAND RAPIDS PUBLIC MUSEUM

272 Pearl St. Northwest
Grand Rapids, MI 49504
(616) 456-3977 | www.grmuseum.org
The Grand Rapids Museum is a world-class facility. It has an excellent educational presentation and is worth the trip. Combine it with an overnight in a nearby state park, and you'll have some happy campers at the end of the weekend. The museum is 110 miles from Ann Arbor.

GRAND TRAVERSE LIGHTHOUSE

15500 North Lighthouse Point Rd.
Northport, MI 49670
(231) 386-7195 | www.grandtraverselighthouse.com
The lighthouse was built in 1858 and has done more than stand the test of time. It has been a beacon of light on dark nights to help guide the way home. Be the dad who helps bring the world of history to life. The lighthouse is 220 miles from Ann Arbor.

GREAT LAKES MARITIME CENTER

The 51 Water St.
Vantage Point
Port Huron, MI 48060
(810) 985-4817 | www.achesonventure.com
The Great Lakes region has a rich history. The Maritime Center offers many educational opportunities for dads and their children about the past and the present.

GREAT LAKES SHIPWRECK MUSEUM

18335 North Whitefish Point Rd.
Paradise, MI 49768
(888) 492-3747 | www.shipwreckmuseum.org
Michigan's oldest active lighthouse also doubles as a museum on the shores of Lake Superior. The museum is filled with history and is specifically dedicated to the perils of maritime travel on the Great Lakes.

HENRY FORD ESTATE

4901 Evergreen Rd.
Dearborn, MI 48128
(313) 593-5592 | www.henryfordestate.org
Fair Lane in Dearborn is where Henry Ford worked his magic. Be the dad who knows where history and pure genius collided. Henry's home is 25 miles from Ann Arbor.

JUNGLE JAVA

3900 Jackson Rd.
Ann Arbor, MI 48103
(734) 786-1340 | www.junglejavaplay.com
Be the dad who took his children on a safari. Jungle Java is the perfect getaway right in the city. This fun center has a separate safe area designed for children called the "Toddler Safari" and an area for adults, too.

KALAMAZOO NATURE CENTER

7000 North Westnedge Ave.
Kalamazoo, MI 49009
(269) 381-1574 | www.naturecenter.org
Be the dad who leads the way. The Nature Center has 11 miles of hiking trials and tons of indoor and outdoor exhibits. This is a camping/hiking trip with an education twist. The Nature Center is about 100 miles from Ann Arbor.

KOKOMOS FAMILY FUN CENTER

5200 Kokomo Dr.
Saginaw, MI 48604
(989) 797-5656 | www.kokomos.com
Kokomos is a must-once-do for all cool dads...twice if you are really cool. Kokomos is a cornucopia of exciting things to do inside and outside. The fun center is located about 100 miles from Ann Arbor.

LASER QUEST

33800 Gratiot Ave.
Detroit, MI 48035
(810) 790-5555 | www.laserquest.com
Laser Quest is an exciting game, and one where even young kids can often outcompete their WonderDad! The field of play is a large multi-leveled arena complete with specialty lighting, fog and heart-pounding music.

THE LOST CITY

12330 James St.
Holland Town Center
Holland, MI 49424
(616) 396-6746 | www.the-lostcity.com
The Lost City is a perfect rainy day destination. Be the dad who knows how to party by planning the best birthday party ever. The Lost City is about 120 miles from Ann Arbor.

MACKINAW TROLLEY TOURS

P.O. Box 358
Mackinaw City, MI 49701
(231) 436-7812 | www.mackinawtrolley.com
Be the dad who takes his children on the ride through history. Climb aboard as the tour narrates the history of Fort Michilimackinac, the Mackinaw Bridge, Father Marquette's Mission, and the Grave Site at St. Ignace. Mackinaw is nearly 250 miles from Ann Arbor, so its best to combine this with other activities!

MINIBEAST MUSEUM & EDUCATIONAL CENTER

6907 West Grand River Ave.
Lansing, MI 48910
(517) 886-0630 | www.michigan.org
This place is considered a Zooseum and incorporates all of the greatest attributes of a zoo and a museum. The learning center is devoted to the study of mini-beasts (macro invertebrate animals, like insects). All science geeks and those who just like science are encouraged to make the trip.

MOBILE LASER KOMBAT

911 Bills Ln.
St. Johns, MI 48879
(989) 292-0369 | www.mobilelaserkombat.com
Why just stop at playing Call of Duty, Halo or Medal of Honor on the latest Xbox. Instead, be the superhero who knows where his kids can climb inside and participate in a live video game (without actually being fragged). Mobile Laser Kombat is only 70 miles from Ann Arbor. Laser Tag is fun and safe, and great game that Dads and kids can compete directly in.

MOTOWN HISTORICAL MUSEUM

2648 West Grand Blvd.

Detroit, MI 48208

(313) 875-2264 | www.motownmuseum.com

Detroit gave birth to an entire generation of music. Be the dad who takes his kids on a walk down memory lane. You never know, your children might be very interested in the tunes you and mom listened and danced to. The museum and a world of musical history are only a half hour drive from Ann Arbor. At the very least they'll recognize the samples in the latest hip-hop tunes.

MUSEUM OF CONTEMPORARY ART DETROIT-MOCAD

4454 Woodward Ave.

Detroit, MI 48201

(313) 832-6622 | www.mocadetroit.org

Every hero wants to add a little culture to the lives of children. This is the perfect opportunity to make that happen. The MOCAD is nestled in the heart of Detroit's cultural community and has plenty of public programs, musical performances, and educational reading activities for children. It's only a short trip from Ann Arbor.

NELIS DUTCH VILLAGE

12350 James St.

Holland, MI 49424

(616) 396-1475 | www.dutchvillage.com

There's nothing better than bumper cars on a Saturday afternoon. Well, Nelis is a 10-acre theme park complete with a family petting zoo that's only 120 miles from Ann Arbor.

NOTTAWA FRUIT FARM

24878 M-86

Sturgis, MI 49091

(269) 467-7719 | www.nottawafruitfarm.com

There's nothing like getting it fresh from the farm. This family-owned business specializes in home-grown produce and family fun.

90

OUTDOOR DISCOVERY CENTER-MACATAWA GREENWAY

A-4214 56th St.
Holland, MI 49423
(616) 393-9453 | www.outdoordiscoverycenter.org
Getting back to nature takes on a whole new meaning at the ODC. Be the dad who knows where to go to see nature and wildlife up close. Be sure to bring a camera, there's plenty to photograph. The ODC is 126 miles from Ann Arbor.

PUMP IT UP

46090 Michigan Ave.
Canton, MI 48188
(734) 495-1222 | www.pumpitupparty.com
When all you have to do is bring a car load of happy children to a party place, it's easy to be the hero. Pump It Up is an inflatable party zone where children can have memorable birthday parties. Be the dad who knows how to throw a memorable kids' party. Canton is only 20 miles from Ann Arbor.

RIVERSIDE ROLLER-SKATING ARENA

36635 Plymouth Rd.
Livonia, MI 48150
(734) 421-3540 | www.riversidearena.com
I remember learning to skate growing up and how much fun I had. Be the dad who delivers on the fun. The Riverside Arena offers open skate times as well as classes dedicated to helping beginners learn to stake. Preschool skate classes are offered every Wednesday. Livonia is only 26 miles from Ann Arbor.

SILVER LAND SAND DUNES

2332 Comfort Dr.
Hart, MI 48420
(800) 874-3982 | www.thinkdunes.com
Be the dad who knows where all of the coolest beaches are. These beaches have miles and miles of rolling sand and dunes. This is the place to go. It's nestled just a few miles west of US-31 between Muskegon and Pentwater, Michigan, about 75 miles from Ann Arbor.

SKATELAND WEST

37550 Cherry Hill
Westland. MI 48185
(734) 326-2800 | www.skatelandwest.com
Learning to skate is like riding a bike. Be the dad who has roller skating in common with his children. The skating rink is only 15 miles from Ann Arbor.

SLEEPING BEAR DUNES

9922 Front St.

Empire, MI 49630

(231) 326-5134 | www.home.nps.gov/slbe

Be the dad who has the inside scoop. Sleeping Bear Dunes is a breath tak-ing family getaway. The Dunes also include two islands with a combined 60 miles of postcard scenic shorelines. The dunes are only 250 miles from Ann Arbor.

SPLASH UNIVERSE

100 Whitetail Dr.

Dundee, MI 48161

(877) 752-7482 | www.splashuniverse.com

Be the dad who lets his child enjoy outdoor fun inside. The water park is only 20 miles from Ann Arbor and is known for year-round fun.

SOO LOCKS BOAT TOURS

1157 East Portage Ave.

Marie, MI 49783

1 (800) 432-6301 | www.soolocks.com/index/phtml

Pay a visit to Michigan's oldest city, Sault Ste. Marie, and tour the interna-tional shoreline of the world's largest waterway traffic system. Soo Locks is one of the great wonders of the world and is 472 kilometers from Ann Arbor.

THUNDER FALLS FAMILY WATER PARK

1028 South Nicolet

Mackinaw City, MI 49701

(231) 436-6000 | www.thunderfallswaterpark.com

I've had the pleasure of traveling up north on several occasions. Twice I've passed through Mackinaw City. The breath-taking views in and around the Mackinaw Bridge is well worth the journey. But the water park is an added bonus! However, from a child's point of view it would be the reason to travel 400 kilometers from Ann Arbor. The 20-acre water theme park has 20 world class water slides and Michigan's best wave pool.

TRI-CITIES HISTORICAL MUSEUM

200 Washington Ave.

Grand Haven, MI 49417

(616) 842-0700 | www.tri-citiesmuseum.org

Buckle up and get ready to travel back in time. This museum offers its visi-tors a window seat to a time machine. Visitors can view Northwest Ottawa County as it existed in the past.

WALTER P. CHRYSLER MUSEUM

1 Chrysler Dr.
Detroit, MI 48326
(248) 944-0460 | www.chryslerheritage.com
It's important to understand the past so that you can better understand the present and the future. Children can learn about history through interactive kiosk stations and educational films. The Chrysler Museum is only 58 kilometers from Ann Arbor.

ZEHNDER'S SPLASH VILLAGE

1365 South Main St.
Frankenmuth, MI 48734
(800) 863-7999 | www.zehnders.com
Zehnder's Splash Village is a great water park, with features for kids of every age, and their WonderDads, within a two hour drive from Ann Arbor. It's a perfect place for a family vacation or day trip.

ABOUT THE AUTHOR

John Isaac Benjamin had the great fortune to be the son of a WonderDad, a man dedicated to being there for his son and making lasting memories together. It was his WonderMom, though, who gave him his start in writing, reading classics aloud to him in his youth and encouraging him to follow his passion. He owes this book to both of them, and wrote it to enable other dads to be WonderDads for their kids. John graduated from the University of Connecticut with a degree in Journalism in 1982, and has worked for newspapers around the country as a writer and editor. He currently lives in Ann Arbor.

THANK YOUS FROM THE AUTHOR

Special thanks to my brother-in-law, Donald Ward, for his help in researching this book. His quick and well-considered responses and guidance proved invaluable. Thank you to Greg Kelley. He has always been willing to lend a hand or jump in when needed. His help in researching this book was greatly appreciated. Finally, a big thank you to Jessica Black of the Ann Arbor Parks and Recreation Department. Her help with researching Ann Arbor parks proved very valuable.